Buji and Me

7 Lessons from the Dog Who Rescued Me

WeNDY KeLLY, M.Ed.

Art by "Blondie" cartoonist

MEDALLION

P R E S S

Medallion Press, Inc.

Printed in USA

Published 2011 by Medallion Press, Inc.

The MEDALLION PRESS LOGO
is a registered trademark of Medallion Press, Inc.

Written with Rick Killian, Killian Creative, Boulder, Colorado.
www.killiancreative.com

Typeset in Adobe Garamond Pro
Printed in the United States of America
ISBN: 9781605421117

10 9 8 7 6 5 4 3 2
First Edition

DEDICATION

To the memory of my mom and dad:

Your love and positive energy continue to inspire me every day.

To Buji:

Thank you for teaching me to listen to those who needed to be heard, myself included.

To the two-legged and four-legged teachers, past and present:

Thank you for being the light on my journey's way.

To the late great "Macho Man" Randy:

Thank you and Lynn for your love and support. You taught me how to rise to my own occasion. "Oooooooooooh yeahhhhhhh-hhhhhhh!"

To my family and friends:

Thank you for loving me beyond reason for all the right reasons.

To Helen:

Thank you for believing in my message and helping me share it with others.

To my Anam Cara:

You have been a "home" to me always . . .

Understanding both ends of the leash—
Our end of the leash:
 A place to belong, to simply be,
 To love and be loved, and forever be free.
Their end of the leash:
 To belong, to behave as bred,
 To lead, to be safe, to be fed.

—Pet Peeves Animal Training Inc. mantra

CONTENTS

FOREWORD

When I met and got to know Wendy Kelly, I immediately recognized something in her that I know about myself. Animals communicate. We listen.

Like Wendy, I learned just how clearly and intelligently animals can tell us what they know and want us to know. The following is how I learned.

Several years ago, I had a serious stroke. Mercifully, I recovered with no neurological deficits, but psychologically I was devastated. I had just finished a long course of chemotherapy for my second bout with breast cancer and feared illness was now a fact of life that would seriously slow down my extremely active lifestyle. I became so depressed I couldn't even get out of bed. And then Simone entered my life.

My best friend and horse trainer, Ruth, knew exactly how to help me. It would definitely involve an animal. I adore my horses and have always considered them the greatest of spiritual healers, but she couldn't get me out of bed to get me to the barn, and she couldn't get a horse up the stairs to my room. A pitiful meowing in the bushes in her front yard solved her problem and saved my sanity.

With my daughter's aid, Ruth rounded up the six feral kittens, put them in a box, brought them to my room, and put the box on the foot of my bed. Pitiful mewling immediately perked me up. I sat up so I could pull the kittens closer and have a look at them. But one was already up and over the edge, climbing out. A tiny gray tabby. She landed on my leg and ran on it straight up into my lap. She didn't stop there. Reaching up toward my chest with her front paws, she begged to be held. A feral kitten. Her siblings, terrified, remained curled in their box.

I obliged the kitten and tucked her into my embrace. She started to purr.

Eventually, the other kittens were moved to another part of the house to begin their lives as more of my adopted feline children. Simone, as she was now called, never left my bedroom. Seldom since she crawled into my arms has she left my side.

Buji and Me

Simone has a gift. One night with her and the next morning I nearly bounded out of bed. In following weeks, she continued to demonstrate her talents. When I was upset and my blood pressure, always a problem, was elevated, Simone would climb into my arms, purr, and touch me, and my pressure was demonstrably lowered.

I told Wendy about my remarkable cat. She asked if I would like her to assess Simone for therapy work. Yes. I knew she would pass, which she did. With flying colors. She subsequently earned her badge and vest and now travels about the country with me doing her life's work.

Simone always knows when someone is in need. And she alerts me.

At horse shows, occasionally when I greet a friend, Simone will try to climb out of my arms and into my friend's. I always allow her. Then she does her job, purring and touching, and reaching a human soul. Tears follow. And confessions of recent trauma or heartache. And when Simone climbs back into my arms, I know she has helped to heal another heart. It is always affirmed by the person healed.

If we are in a crowd and Simone detects someone who needs her, she alerts me by meowing insistently until I spot what she has seen. Once it was a woman in a wheelchair at a public event. Simone moaned until I brought her within reach of the disabled older woman, who looked up at me questioningly.

"My cat, Simone, is special," I told her simply. "She would like to give you a gift. Is it all right if she touches you?"

The woman nodded slowly. Her four attendant family members crowded around us anxiously. Simone reached out and gently touched her arm.

"Ohhhh," the woman sighed. Then she smiled. Grinned. Beamed. Her family burst into tears.

"I'm so sorry," I said quickly. "Are you all right? What's wrong?"

"Mom," a young woman said, "my mother, she . . . she hasn't smiled in months."

Simone and the older woman enjoyed a good, long cuddle. She finally left with her family, not only smiling but laughing with joy.

Communication of the heart. More than words can ever express.

Listen to them. Hear them.

Let this wonderful book help you learn how.

—Helen A Rosburg

INTRODUCTION

"Ask the animals, and they will teach you."
🐾 Job 12:7, NIV

In the twenty years that I have worked as an applied animal behaviorist, I've discovered an amazing truth: pets have more to teach us than we have to teach them. Their perspectives, unencumbered by the busyness of human existence, tend to be more focused on what is really important in life. They fully participate in their relationships, always expect the best out of every situation, and never get too little sleep. With animals there's no pretense, no excuse, no baggage, no worries concerning what happened yesterday or anxieties about what might happen tomorrow. They simply live every minute to its fullest.

I believe that if we take the time to listen, our pets can offer us some valuable keys to getting the most out of this earthly existence. If we will simply pay attention, our pets can be guides to being, well, better beings. How do I know? My dog, Buji, taught me—and all he had to do to get my attention was save my life.

For pets, there are no prerequisites to getting the most out of life. Animals do happiness well because they know how to simply be. It is never about how they will be happy when they get a certain thing or accomplish a certain task or get that next promotion. They celebrate wherever they are with everything that is within them. They know that fulfillment is not a destination to labor toward but exists all around us every day: all we have to do is embrace it. Pets are content to enjoy each step of life's journey. They do whatever is before them with all their hearts, and just by being around them we are lucky to catch a bit of their joy in that moment.

In the following chapters I want to share with you what Buji and many other animals have taught me over the years about living life to its fullest. As I have worked with two-legged and four-legged animals alike, I have seen the principles I am about to share with you bring fulfillment and satisfaction. I have summed these up in what I call Buji's seven lessons: discoveries I have made along the way to help humans and pets in the arts of healing and personal growth. The principles incorporate what I have found to be the dynamic, life-changing force that occurs when we allow our pets to become our teachers. It's a philosophy that, once embraced, is sure to wag your soul.

While we will explore each of these principles in depth in the chapters to follow, I want to briefly introduce them here so that you can begin to recognize them in your own pet as you read this book. My hope is that they will sprout into life-enhancing guidelines for you as you grow in the days, weeks, and years to come. Buji was my tipping point: the bark that finally broke through to reveal these seven secrets to living a *pawsitive* life.

1. Our pets can teach us how to *be here now.* They are open to the endless possibilities in every moment and never come with an agenda. From a pet's perspective, being is as important as doing. Their minds, bodies, and spirits share a balanced awareness in each and every moment.

2. Our pets can teach us how to *be true.* They are congruent and true to their emotions and the emotions of those around them. Their behaviors always match their thoughts and feelings. They never hide behind layers of falsehoods or rely on carefully crafted façades regardless of the circumstance.

3. Our pets can teach us how to *be aware.* They are able to perceive life as it truly is. They are free from the

pull that judgments, perspectives, and egos have on bending the reality we experience. The reality they see is as real as they are in each and every moment of their lives.

🐾 4.   Our pets can teach us how to *be focused*. Pets are naturally able to access and utilize the power of intention. They are instinctively good at focusing their attention on what they want without being overly concerned about how they will get it. Pets enact the law of intention, which is as real as the law of gravity. Simply put, thoughts create things.

🐾 5.   Our pets can teach us how to *be light*. They don't concern themselves with past hurts or grudges but come to every moment with an open mind and heart. Their lighthearted nature enables them to connect fully with others in moments of pure joy, spontaneity, and fun. Traveling light allows them to spread that light to others.

🐾 6.   Pets can teach us how to *be kind* without expectation or condition. They know the power of what I call *overstanding*. This is the highest level of understanding, which goes beyond merely knowing what another feels but involves accepting and connecting with another from his unique perspective. It involves the act of helping unconditionally. If a dog has ever rested her head in your lap and just seemed to know about your bad day, then you have been what I call *overstood*.

Buji and Me

🐾7.   Our pets can teach us how to *be one with love*.
They recognize and embrace the universal love that connects us all and brings us home, a place where everyone
is part of the pack in the journey to wholeness, contentment, and true happiness.

When people ask me about my approach to working
with animals, I summarize it by simply saying, "I listen
to the animals and teach people to understand their messages." That's why I am not so much a *pet whisperer* as I
am a *pet listener*.

I have come to realize that if we will listen to our pets,
if we will watch and learn, our pets will teach us how to be
whole. Through our interactions and relationships with
them, they will bring out the potential within each of us
to be happy and healthy; they will teach us about spiritual-
ity and about being home in a world that can seem harsh
and unforgiving. If we pay attention, our pets can help
us to stay on the right path toward knowing and becoming complete and fulfilled beings. They will teach us how
to love and be loved, belong and connect, and be in the
moment rather than going through the motions only to
wake up later and realize we have forgotten to live. They
can help us fully be what we were placed on the earth to
be, if we will just stop and pay attention.

I'm excited to share with you what I have learned from one unforgettable companion, Buji, as well as the many animal teachers in my life. Our pets know the path; the universe has built it into them. Are you ready to embark on the journey?

1
Embark on the Journey

*When you want to learn something about yourself, start by
listening first and barking last.*

🐾 Buji

Something miraculous happens when we step outside ourselves enough to connect with an animal.
It is as if somehow, even if only for an instant, we
come into alignment with the way things are supposed
to be. When we do, we find our place. In that moment,
we get a glimpse of what was intended when the earth
came into existence, the harmonious occupation of time
and space for various species together, each bringing out
the best in the other, partnering on the great adventure of life,
blessing every day with fulfillment and joy, making a difference one little ripple in the great pond of the universe at a time.

Over the last twenty-five years, science has quantified
the significance of the connection between people and
their pets. Research has shown that interacting with

animals, whether petting a cat, playing fetch with a dog, or watching a goldfish swim in a bowl, raises our serotonin and dopamine levels (the neurotransmitters in our brains that signal well-being).

One study showed that stockbrokers with high blood pressure who adopted a dog or cat had lower blood pressure readings during stressful situations than did those who had no pets at all. Several studies have shown that heart patients who have pets tend to live longer than those who don't.[1] A Study in Belfast found that dog owners suffered less from sicknesses, had lower cholesterol levels and lower blood pressure in addition to increased survival rates after suffering a heart attack.[2] A ten-year study of four thousand three hundred Americans revealed that owning a cat could cut your risk of heart attack by almost one-third.[3]

There is no question in my mind that pets increase our well-being and longevity, and sharing our lives with animal companions does something beyond what's measurable. Interacting with animals, particularly ones that have become our pets, inspires wholeness within us, and the connection has a spiritual dimension as well.

The power of this connection is woven into the very fabric of our beings. Traveling life's journey with an animal companion contributes to a full and happy life. If we will pay attention, we can catch a glimpse of the universe smiling back at us through the eyes of our pets. It's as if somehow, even if only for an instant, we come into alignment with the way things are truly supposed to be. We find our place in the universe where being and belonging have always been our home.

It is not always easy to explain, but it is tangible: pets have a way of making us better at being human and humane if we will let them. As we move through life, it's a clue the universe gives us about why we are here and what we are supposed to do to make this journey worthwhile for all.

Meeting Buji was the spark that helped me awaken.

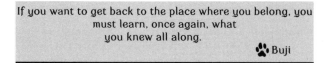

If you want to get back to the place where you belong, you must learn, once again, what you knew all along.

🐾 Buji

All my life, I have sought out the companionship of the natural world around me. As a child, I befriended mammals, birds, bugs, and trees. It may sound strange, but they all made me feel like I belonged, that I was a part of something bigger, that I could understand and be understood without uttering a word or doing a thing, that I was complete just by being in their presence. It is something I still feel today.

This connection has led me to my current path. It is why I chose to work with animals—or why they choose to work with me. Perhaps it is my Native American heritage that runs deep in my soul and reminds me of the energy we share with all living things, the energy that welcomes us home unconditionally, regardless of who we are or what we do in this time and space. It is this connection that shapes my journey and has undoubtedly been the source of my sanity and wholeness.

Animals can teach us that we belong to something greater than ourselves. Maybe this is why I have always known that at the heart of our existence, we are all one.

> Breathe. Let go. And remind yourself that this very moment is the only one you know you have for sure.
> 🐾 Oprah Winfrey

I remember spending hours of my childhood waiting and hoping to get a brief glimpse of understanding into the animals around me. I would round up the dogs in my neighborhood for a town meeting of sorts just so I could study their interactions.

BUji and Me

I learned that I could accurately predict their behavior in future meetings: who would sniff whom, who would stake claim to a toy or territory with hackles up, who would make friends with blurred tails while others sheepishly displayed their soft underbellies.

I also "borrowed" my canine friends for one-on-one meetings. I delighted in teaching them a trick or two and returning them home with their heads as full as their bellies and their tails wagging, to the joyful surprise of their families. Like a thirsty sponge, I soaked up every moment as I learned to understand and hear what my animal friends were communicating.

It wasn't just dogs who captured my attention. Some days I could be found on all fours peering closely into the volcanic mound of an ant colony. I would take my primary color paint set and color code individual ants so that I could track their business matters and social interactions of the day, all of which I would carefully document in my double-lined writing tablet after paying for my colorful intrusion in fine grains of sugar currency.

There was not a creature in my neighborhood who escaped my curious gaze. Tadpoles, birds, squirrels, and spiders got equal attention in my backyard summer research projects.

I guess, in all fairness, you could say I was a bit different from the other kids in my neighborhood. As a matter of fact, you could say the same of me now, and that would be true. As a student of life, I know one thing for sure: I am grateful to be surrounded every day by the greatest of all teachers.

> This process of the good life is not, I am convinced, a life for the faint-hearted. It involves the stretching and growing of becoming more and more of one's potentialities. It involves the courage to be. It means launching oneself fully into the stream of life.
> 🐾 Carl Rogers

All my life, I have been drawn to animals, perhaps instinctively knowing that I needed them to teach me, heal me, and help me learn how to heal myself and others. Perhaps being an animal behaviorist is what I was meant to be all along, but I didn't set out to become one.

I started my career as a psychotherapist, working with college athletes as well as students and faculty, in the University Counseling Center at Wichita State University. Having been a collegiate athlete myself, I knew the importance of the mind-body connection in achieving outstanding performance. I routinely took clients through hypnotherapy, solution-focused therapy, and creative visualization exercises.

BUji and Me

I had track athletes lie on the floor, close their eyes, and run their races entirely in their minds. I would time them with a stopwatch, and astonishingly enough they would repeatedly finish within hundredths of a second of their actual race times. I was amazed to witness the accuracy and power of the mind. Not only were they able to run their mental races with precision, but by utilizing the power of their minds they were able to shave seconds off their actual performance times. That may not sound like a lot, but in track one second is often the difference between first place and not placing at all.

Additionally, baseball players who were in batting slumps improved after visualizing hitting home runs: feeling, hearing, and seeing their ultimate success at the plate in their mind's eye.

It all worked like a charm but still failed to answer some of the deeper questions that constantly poked at my mind. It turns out that the mind is a very sharp tool and an excellent servant, though a terrible master. We can think ourselves into feeling good, miserable, scared, successful, or unsuccessful: the possibilities are endless.

My dad, a wise man with a keen wit and a knack for saying the right thing at the right time, used to tell me before I would line up for a grueling quarter-mile sprint over hurdles, "Wendy, you're better than you think. You run. I'll think."

He was wise beyond any education or degree one could attain, and he was right. When I let go of worrying, second-guessing, and hounding myself about my performance, I was able to excel by being in the moment and allowing my mind to be my servant, not my master.

I remember the story my dad once told me about Roger Bannister, the first athlete to break the four-minute mile, which many considered an impossible feat at the time. When the media asked Bannister how he was able to do it when no one else ever could, he responded, "I refused to believe that it wasn't possible." Our minds can create wings or barriers for us depending upon what we choose to think.

> Minds are like parachutes—they only function when they are open.
> 🐾 Thomas Dewar

The more I worked with athletes in this way, the more I wanted to learn about people beyond how to improve their performance in athletic arenas. I wanted to know, really know, what made them tick far beyond the pace of any stopwatch. I wanted to understand the concept of being versus doing. I wondered how behavior plays a role in our happiness and how we arrive at defining happiness in the first place. Of course, this was much trickier to grasp and even more difficult to measure.

This curiosity and the nagging necessity to answer these questions was the reason I became a psychotherapist. Humans fascinated me, and I wanted to contribute something that would change lives for the better and also find the answers I so desperately sought.

So I started out at the university, then worked for the Cayman Islands government (a story I will tell you in chapter five), then settled in Florida to work as a psychotherapist. I loved helping people uncover, unravel, and mend the fabric of what made them who they were, while encouraging them to be what they hoped to become. This was what I was meant to do, or so I thought.

It's time to trust my instincts. Close my eyes, and leap!
🐾 Stephen Schwartz

One day a cat named Brie came into my life. She was a brown, black, and white calico with a dark furry spot on her nose that looked much like a sailboat in a sea of white fur. She was a shelter cat, a stray who couldn't find a home. I regularly went to visit her at the shelter in Grand Cayman until one day she communicated that she wanted me to take her to my home, so I did.

Soon Brie started hanging around my office while I worked. As it happened, one of my clients who was sitting in the waiting room scooped Brie up and placed her on her lap. When I came out to greet my client, even before I had a chance to speak, I saw something in her that I hadn't in all the weeks I had known her.

As she sat stroking Brie's soft fur, completely absorbed in the moment, I saw wholeness. I continued to watch her, unnoticed, as she tilted her head and leaned forward to listen more closely to the rhythm of Brie's purr. She smiled as her fingers traced the outline of the sailboat spot on Brie's nose. In that moment, she was happy, genuinely happy, and it had nothing to do with psychotherapy and everything to do with connecting with this purring bundle of fur. She was completely immersed in the moment in which everything was right with her and the world.

Brie had helped this woman connect in the present to be here now. She learned what she always knew instinctively but had forgotten along the way: that wellness is a state one achieves not by doing but by simply being.

After witnessing this magic, I realized that the healing connection I have always felt with animals was something others could feel as well. I began to explore the use of animals in the field of psychotherapy. Through my research, I found that animals had a profound effect on our physical, mental, spiritual, and emotional well-being. I discovered that people were starting to recognize and tap into the healing energy that animals have to offer.

It all made perfect sense to me. Being with animals allows us to simply be. Somehow hang-ups get shelved when we pick up a cat or watch a gerbil running on a wheel. We are drawn into the here and now, and the here and now is a very healthy place to be.

> There is no psychiatrist in the world like a puppy licking your face.
>
> 🐾 Ben Williams

I began working with animals in my spare time, volunteering at the Humane Society and the Society for the Prevention of Cruelty to Animals (SPCA). I studied animal behavior with the same passion I had studied the cognitive behavioral processes in humans. I began training animals in shelters so they would be more likely to be adopted. I also learned how to prepare proper candidates for hearing, sight, balance, or emotional assist canines. These therapy animals provided emotional support and healing to those in rest homes, hospital wards, and other institutions. It was miraculous to witness how they used their charms to help those who most needed their unconditional companionship.

As I observed these pets interacting with humans, I learned new and different ways to facilitate growth and understanding. I began to recognize a natural congruency with animals that was infectious. As people allowed themselves to connect fully with animals, the barriers that I had found so difficult to breach as a psychotherapist seemed to melt away with ease. People acted emotionally healthier, and the more they interacted with the animals, the more they seemed to be able to tap into an ability to heal themselves, something which had always been available to them but had seemed just beyond their reach. When they let go of the distraction of trying to fix themselves, they became aware that wellness had been there all along: a constant companion waiting in the here and now for an opportunity to emerge and reunite them with wholeness.

As an animal behaviorist, I never have to guess what an animal is thinking or feeling because they show me freely in the honesty of their behaviors. Animals live truthfully. They are always genuine and congruent inside and out. Pets are real and never apologize for it. They are not attached to outcomes or events. They hope and want, but they can just as easily let go. Pets live their inner world and their outer world seamlessly, which allows them to plug in to a way of being that celebrates similarities as well as differences. There's no bottling up of emotions, burying hurts under years of pretending that everything is fine, no lying to self and others. Animals, unlike humans, never pretend.

This congruent nature of an animal's behavior facilitates understanding, and understanding leads to healing. An animal's behavior always mirrors the inner workings of the mind and heart. For example, when a dog feels threatened, she snarls. When a cat feels content, he purrs. When a horse feels spry, she gallops with her head held high and her mane whipping in the breeze. Birds will dance and squawk to show they are happy or sound an alarm if it fits the occasion. There is no façade between animals and their world. Pets don't put on airs or repress motives or feelings.

The truth doesn't require many words. In fact, it requires no words at all. Animals live harmoniously with what is in and around them. Instinct tells them they are connected to it all.

> One of the most appreciated qualities of animals is that they are beyond language. That they feel but do not require conversation is a great relief to most people.
> 🐾Mary Allen

As these realizations—my initial noodling that would be the groundwork for this book—were coming together, I decided to incorporate pets into my clients' therapy sessions. The animals helped the clients to focus on being well rather than on what was not working in their lives. It was in perfect sync with my solution-focused approach to working with clients in psychotherapy.

It is a simple behavioral principle that whatever you focus on, you will get more of. If you focus on and reward a wanted behavior in a pet, then the pet will repeat that behavior more often. If you ignore it, then you will get less of that behavior. Similarly, clients who learned to understand and embrace a solution-focused model instead of a problem-focused model were quick to see healthy thinking paving the way toward healing.

To help clients start thinking with a solution-focused perspective and to halt their steady march down the problem-focused path, I would ask them what is called the miracle question: "If you went to sleep tonight and the problems you have right now were gone when you woke up the next morning, how would you know a miracle had happened? How would your life be different? What would people be saying to you? How would you look? How would you feel? What would you be doing?"

By focusing on being healthy rather than on not being sick, we will begin to find better solutions for ourselves. Naturally, we will begin to heal, become whole, and literally live the life we imagine.

> Happiness is a how, not a what; a talent, not an object.
> 🐾 Hermann Hesse

One of the four principles I use in working with animals and people is Thorndike's law of effect, which states, "Behaviors that are reinforced tend to increase in frequency." This principle is based on positive reinforcement: rewarding the subject in a manner that is meaningful to them when they engage in the desired behavior. Following this principle in training animals, I focus on reinforcement and not on correction. The axiom is "you get more of what you focus on."

It has been well documented that correction-based training is not an effective means for fostering any desired target behavior but rather produces fallout behaviors that are undesirable. Most importantly, correction-based training does not teach the animal the desired behavior in the first place. The principle of Thorndike's law is an effective method for shaping behaviors that are desired by incrementally rewarding "close approximations" toward the end target behavior. It is far more effective to catch a mammal engaging in the "right" behavior and reward it than to catch the mammal doing something "undesirable" and correct it. Attention in and of itself is a reward, regardless of whether that attention is negative or positive. Behaviors that we would like to extinguish are best ignored.

Thorndike's Law works for any mammal, whether a dog, dolphin, horse, or mouse. The animal learns very quickly which behaviors are rewarded and which behaviors are not. This involves a good deal of patience on the part of the trainer but is highly effective and ensures that a positive relationship is maintained.

Buji and Me

It is my belief that the method should always match the mission. If you want a positive relationship with your pet, then the manner in which you interact should be positive as well. Training should always be enjoyed at both ends of the leash. Great leaders demonstrate in their actions that they are kind, consistent, and patient and that they will always choose motivation over manipulation. When you are a leader worthy of that title, then you will discover that most any animal, whether two-legged or four-legged, is more than happy to follow you.

> Be content with what you have; rejoice in the way things are. When you realize there is nothing lacking, the whole world belongs to you.
>
> 🐾 Lao Tzu

When we focus on what is wrong in our lives, we pull more of what we don't want into our experiences, or at best we get really good at telling others what is wrong. Focusing on past hurts will not lessen their impact, because we get more of whatever we focus on, good or bad.

When we arrive at the realization that the only time we have ever lived is now, we are able to render our past hurts or our future fears powerless over our present existence. Animals understand the power of living every moment in the moment with all that a moment has to offer.

It is helpful for us to let go of the past in order to welcome what is good in the present. Then we are able to imagine a life that is healthier, happier, and more fulfilling than we first dreamed possible. It is the power of imagination that enables us to summon the energy necessary for creation. And it is this energy that helps us be all that we ever hoped to become.

The more you focus on something, the more of it you get. Our minds are always listening to what we say and working to bring those things into our lives. If we want positive things to happen, then we need to think positively. The more negative our overall demeanor, the more negativity life will seem to bring us.

> A Native American elder once described his own inner struggles in this manner: "Inside of me there are two dogs. One of the dogs is mean and evil. The other dog is good. The mean dog fights the good dog all the time." When asked which dog wins, he reflected for a moment and replied, "The one I feed the most."
> 🐾George Bernard Shaw

Being around pets helps us naturally focus on the positive. The more I worked with pets in my clinic, the healthier it felt.

BUji and Me

It turned out that training animals offered me a better path to changing people's lives than being a psychotherapist ever had.

In fact, when I realized pets were essential to health and wellness, I decided to change careers. I left my job as the director of a counseling center and opened Pet Peeves Animal Training, my own animal therapy practice in Clearwater, Florida. I dedicated myself to working full-time with pets and, thus, their parents. This gave me new inroads to continue to train rescue dogs, service pets, and therapy animals and provided me with a whole gamut of ways to help people.

My decision to shift careers, though perfectly logical in my own mind, was met with its fair share of raised eyebrows and behind-the-scenes chuckles. When asked my reason, I simply said, "I've discovered that, unlike dogs, people won't change for a biscuit." With the corners of my mouth turning slightly upward, I'd say, "I've never actually tried using this technique with clients, but I'm certain I'm onto something."

Little did I know how much that decision would change my life.

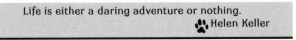

Life is either a daring adventure or nothing.
Helen Keller

It was during one of my forays into the local animal shelter around this transitional time of my life that I met Buji. I first noticed him sitting alone in a kennel, separated from all the other dogs. He was a Staffordshire bull terrier who looked as if he'd had a rough life. His face was marked with cuts and scratches, physical scars that were a testament to a life of abuse and cruelty. He barked and growled as I approached him, jumping viciously at the kennel door. It was startling, but my heart went out to him.

I soon learned that it was impossible for anyone on the staff of the shelter to go near him and that he attacked any dog who approached him. His aggressive behavior had put him on the short list to be euthanized, and he was scheduled to be put down in the next twenty-four hours.

Despite all this, the minute I had set eyes on him, something inside had told me I had to help him. It was the oddest feeling, but I couldn't shake it. Everyone thought he was a dangerous animal, unredeemable and better off exterminated, but every instinct in me said there was hope for him and I needed to save him.

So with the stealthy hands of a magician, I snatched the card off his cage—the one that sealed his demise—and quickly tucked it in my pocket and peeled out of there. He would be spared another day, and that allowed me time to try to understand the strange pull he had on me.

> He has achieved success who has lived well, laughed often and loved much . . . who has left the world better than he found it, whether by an improved poppy, a perfect poem, or a rescued soul.
> 🐾 Bessie Stanley

That night I couldn't sleep as I thought about Buji and what his life must have been like prior to his ending up on the shelter's short list. His scarred muzzle told a story of possibly being forced to fight, exploited at the hands of ill-intentioned humans, and then thrown away.

The notion of bringing a "dangerous" bull terrier home was not one of my most welcome ideas. My roommate had two small Maltipoos, Idgy and Dagney. As the two pairs of trusting eyes stared up at me through fuzzy white fluff, I thought, *How can I consider bringing this dog home and putting them at risk of injury?*

Had I lost my mind? My roommate was certain I had, and secretly so was I.

As I assured her that it would be fine, I so wanted to believe the comforting words I was carefully crafting to persuade her. However, I realized they weren't really reassuring me. Perhaps morning would bring clarity and a bit more sanity or at least a better plan for all concerned.

> The little furry buggers are just deep, deep wells you throw all your emotions into.
> 🐾 Bruce Schimmel

The next morning I walked into the shelter with nervous anticipation. I hoped my card trick from the night prior had worked. I held my breath and rounded the corner to the row of kennels where Buji had been.

My heart sank as I stood in front of an empty kennel. He was gone. I had failed him!

As my tears welled up, I heard a menacing bark two rows away. I ran and slid around the corner as if I were on my way to home plate.

It was him. He was still alive! They had moved him

to sort out his situation and look for the missing card that I had crumpled in my pocket the day before.

I knew then that I had to move quickly. After pulling a few strings, I was signing his papers.

Meanwhile, the shelter staff members were raising their eyebrows.

It didn't matter. He was mine.

Oddly, as I snapped a leash to his collar, he didn't object or even snarl as he had before. Somehow he must have realized this was his last shot at freedom.

I marched somewhat triumphantly out to my car, handling with confidence and pride an animal no one else was able to approach. I let him into the passenger side of my two-seated convertible, a surge of accomplishment filling my soul. I had saved a life. I was the animal rescuer who would save the one all the rest had labeled a lost cause.

> To the world you are a rescue person. To the rescued animal, you are the world.
> 🐾 Unknown

Holding my head high, I felt the eyes of the staff on me as I rounded my car to get into the driver's seat. Buji had been cooperative enough as I had led him out of the shelter, but I should have known it wouldn't be that easy.

Now he decided my car would be his new home to defend and protect with his life. As I put my hand on the latch to open the door, he launched himself against the window, barking ferociously.

I jumped like a startled rabbit, my eyes as wide as dinner plates. I flushed, almost hearing the snickers from inside the shelter. As I crossed to the passenger side, Buji lunged at me again, no less enthusiastic in his determination to keep me out.

A thought occurred to me: *I might never be able to get into my car again.*

Then it began to rain.

For the next half hour or so, circling my car, cajoling, using every trick I had learned during my lifetime of working with animals, I tried to negotiate a way into my car.

For his part, Buji was a blur racing from one window to the other as I circled.

If anyone was really watching from inside, it must have been a hilarious sight: the expert animal behaviorist who knew better than they did about this dog's potential was now trapped outside her car, dripping wet, foiled by the very creature whose cause she had championed.

Buji and Me

It was my first lesson from Buji: humility.

> I am I because my little dog knows me.
> 🐾 Gertrude Stein

After nearly forty-five minutes, I wore Buji down, got into the car, and sheepishly pulled out of the parking lot, hiding behind the steering wheel to avoid the eyes I still felt following my every move. I don't think I have ever had the question *What was I thinking?* pop into my head so many times in such a short period at any other point in my life!

After witnessing his behavior, I first took Buji to the Pet Peeves kennels for the welfare of my pack at home. I knew it would be the best place to start his training. Once he grew more comfortable with me, and I with him, I would take him home. I got him into the kennel without much trouble, but then he guarded it just as he had my car.

Any doubts I had, however, were still overpowered by my desire to help. For some internal reason, I just couldn't give up on him as others had. Something in the universe had drawn me to him.

Even if it seemed crazy, I knew I didn't want him to be put down. I just couldn't give up on him like that. I sensed I needed to help him somehow and that my doing so was just as important to me as it was to him.

> Isn't it wonderful how dogs can win friends and influence people without ever reading a book?
> 🐾 E. C. McKenzie

I believe we as pet parents draw into our lives pets who may have characteristics we aspire to or who will help us heal something in us that is out of alignment.

One of our shortcomings is that we tend to look at situations from our own vantage points but never truly see them. Rather than taking in moments for what they are, we weigh, judge, and sentence them before we truly understand them.

We all have the potential for change and healing built into the very essence of our souls. The truth is that we tend toward being healthy and fulfilled both naturally and spiritually, but pain and hurt can clog that natural flow of energy. We make the mistake of trying to get healthy instead of just being healthy. We don't recognize the true potential or inherent worth of something, whether it's an idea, a conscious being, or a certain set of circumstances. We think we know the outcome before we even engage, and in that process we often give up too soon on ourselves or on someone else. We lose our way.

From my Native American heritage, I've learned that animals are, in many ways, our guides. They show us the way along life's path. While any animal you see may be a sign, I believe it is the animals we pull into our lives who have the most meaning and impact.

I've repeatedly observed that we find the pets (or they find us) who will help us expand our souls in significant ways or, as in my case, who hold a key to some future situation we will be forced to face. As most animals do, Buji had things to teach me about myself.

> Of all the animals, surely the dog is the only one that really shares our life, helps in our work, and has a place in our recreation.
> Ferdinand Mercy

I have never really believed in coincidences. If you've fallen in love with a pet, there is a reason beyond reason.

On a conscious level, I chose Buji because I knew he needed me, but I believe that subconsciously I pulled Buji into my life because I needed him. He had lessons to teach me, things I needed to learn to survive the difficult times ahead.

Though I didn't know it that first day with Buji, he had a lot to share with me. He started by teaching me that "the present" is the gift life wants us to unwrap.

Paws and Reflect

When contemplating any decision, ask yourself these five questions:

🐾 1. Is it what I believe?

🐾 2. Is it necessary?

🐾 3. Will it bring joy to my life?

🐾 4. Will it bring joy to others?

🐾 5. Can I do it with unconditional love?

2

Be Here Now:
The Power of Presence

What does that mean: "too busy today"? Life happens in
the moments that we let ourselves play.
🐾Buji

In the following days, the real work with Buji would
begin. I realized the first thing he needed was to be
able to be comfortable with someone around him. I had
to help him unlearn aggression as a response to anyone
approaching.

My initial perceptions of Buji were more emotions
than observations. I felt his despair at being totally aban-
doned by the world, but I also knew there was something
more to it. As I looked at him, I could perceive that his
aggression wasn't pathological or genetic. I believed that
somewhere along the line he'd learned to use aggression as
a tool to make things better for himself. In his perception,
it was a necessary skill.

For me, it couldn't be about determining whether he was a good or a bad dog. That kind of perspective had gotten him scheduled to be euthanized. Instead, I sought to understand the nature of his behavior, to determine how it had developed. Behaviors are not the problems to be solved. Rather, they are symptoms of previous conditioning.

To see beyond the simple behavior and what it was supposed to accomplish for him, I had to genuinely connect with Buji.

> I bit you on the hand because I couldn't reach your ear for you to hear me.
>
> 🐾 Buji

Lao Tzu stated, "A journey of a thousand miles begins with a single step." What he didn't tell us is that your first step is often your longest leap. In order to modify Buji's aggression, I knew I had to do four things: connect with him to let him know I could be trusted, learn what had inspired his behavior, help him to unlearn the behavior specific to different stimuli, and teach him that his aggressive behavior was no longer necessary in any situation.

It was not a process in which I used my superior human strength and intellect to dominate him and make him submit. It was not a question of my strength of will versus his. I had no desire to break his spirit or do anything that could harm him. The approach required first accepting and understanding the behavior without attaching any judgment to it.

> I know that you believe you understand what you think I said, but I'm not sure you realize that what you heard is not what I meant.
> Robert McCloskey

Before I started training Buji, I stood outside his kennel to study him with the safety of steel and concrete between us. He was an amazing-looking creature with bold yet handsome features. His dark brown eyes, set deep under thick bone and brow, followed my every move with laser-like precision. His jaw was muscular and flared out much beyond the confines of his face. His ears had been clipped, which left him with the appearance of a devilish bull. With his wide neck and broad chest, he reminded me of a canine version of "Macho Man" Randy Savage. He was built to fight. Buji's wrinkled brow, etched with distrust, told me to stay put just outside his kennel for the time being. His body was tattooed with black vertical stripes that stretched tightly over his massive dark brown frame. His muzzle was notched with the impressions that other dogs had left on him. It seemed he had learned to fight to survive and most likely to win the favor of those who didn't deserve him in the first place.

That day and during the three to follow, I waited for Buji to let me know I could approach before I made a move. It may sound strange, but I read books to him so he would grow accustomed to the sound of my voice. I waited for him to meet me in a place where he felt safer than he ever had before.

I waited and watched, and then on day four I sensed he was willing to trust a little more. It was time to take the next step and enter the kennel with him.

It didn't take me long to figure out that Buji used aggression to help him feel safe. So what I had to do was convince him he could be safe without attacking. I needed to create an environment where aggression received no reinforcement, either negative or positive, and where peaceful behavior was rewarded and praised.

My approach was to speak this message to Buji through my actions: "It's a new world you are living in now. I am going to make sure you feel safe no matter how you behave. I am going to let you know that I love your courageous spirit but also that I don't want you to hurt anybody anymore. Don't bite when a simple lip curl might do; don't assault when simply walking away will do. You can be safe without doing that. You don't need those responses anymore. In fact, life is going to be far better without them. Just you wait and see."

With most dogs in such a situation, I would wear protective gear and try to elicit the aggression as part of an assessment so I could observe what triggered it and study the behavioral anatomy of the bite. Something told me not to do that with Buji. I wanted us to establish a no-aggression pact from day one. I wanted a training program that would never threaten the relationship or the courage of Buji's spirit.

An open heart will reach me faster than a raised hand.
🐾 Buji

Working with Buji reinforced my approach to training animals. I am different from traditional train-by-force advocates in that I feel my instructive methods always need to be congruent with the desired outcome and grounded in sound behavioral principles. The methods used should always match the desired mission.

Some trainers will try to extinguish aggression with more aggression. That has never made sense to me. It's like getting emotionally involved in a contest of wills with the animal: *Oh no, you didn't just try to bite me! I'll show you who's boss.*

Instead, I believe the best way to reach an abused and frightened animal is to gently earn his trust so that the fear-based aggression subsides. As a rule, dogs rarely fear what will happen next unless they have learned to do so through exposure to a repeated pattern of pain or abuse or unless they are inexperienced in social situations.

I never use punishment-based techniques like choke chains or shock collars, and I never will. I believe animal training is about trust, kindness, and leadership, and I never want to do anything in my practices that would jeopardize the wonderful spirit of the animal or our positive relationship.

In my opinion, forceful tactics are cruel and archaic. I believe trainers who still employ these methods lack a basic understanding of animal behavior and the proper application of behavioral principles that would otherwise guide them to train positively. I believe some trainers confuse dominance with being domineering, using intimidation and force to establish who's in charge rather than applying a simple understanding of instinctual leadership principles found in the animal kingdom.

Trust must be established through letting the animal know you are trustworthy. If you show pets you are worth following, they will gladly let you lead. To win their approval, you must simply provide direction and rewards congruent with their instinctual paradigm.

When you create an environment that is safe and pleasurable, you increase an animal's capacity to learn. A good relationship is the foundation. Connection is necessary before training can be effective. Once the connection is made, then an agreement is established to move forward in a manner that is rewarding and fun for animal and trainer alike.

I tell my students and clients that I have only two rules for working with animals. Rule number one: always make sure training is enjoyed at both ends of the leash. Rule number two: never forget rule number one.

Establishing a partnership with an animal demands a good deal of patience, but in the end it is worth it for all concerned. For me, it would lead to learning Buji's first lesson: *be here now.*

> Our patience will achieve more than our force.
> 🐾 Edmund Burke

My plan with Buji was very simple. I would spend about twenty minutes several times a day simply going into his kennel and being with him until he accepted my presence. Through my actions, I had to tell him, "I'm not going to hurt you. I'm not going to challenge you. I'm not somebody you have to fight with for a position." I wouldn't try to train anything into or out of him. Instead, I would calmly be there with him until he could calmly be there with me.

The first time I entered Buji's kennel without any protective gear, I knew I risked being bitten. I determined it was a risk I was willing to take. If he bit me, he bit me. I wasn't going to react. I would be there with him fully in the moment. I would not allow him to determine or shape my behavior. No matter what he did, I would respond with kindness. I would model the behavior I wanted out of him. I would ignore the aggressive behavior and reward the behaviors approaching friendliness.

With most animals, during an assessment I can observe and accurately determine future behaviors. With Buji, however, this was not the case. All I knew was that the minute I entered his kennel, he might lunge at me with teeth gnashing or let me in without much resistance just as he had once let me lead him to my car. I would need to take it slow, be aware, and ultimately take a well-planned step forward.

> An integral being knows without going, sees without looking, and accomplishes without doing.
> 🐾 Lao Tzu

As a rule, dogs aren't naturally mean-spirited. If they seem violent or antisocial, if they bite or attack, ninety-nine times out of a hundred it's because they've been in situations where they've learned that a particular behavior benefited them in some way. Much less frequently, there are idiopathic cases in animals who cannot be helped with medication or behavior modification training. These are always sad to see, but I am glad that they are rare.

If you look at the world from your dog's perspective, his teeth are indeed the tools nature has left in his mouth. Some dogs have found that using their teeth aggressively is an effective means to get what they need. The more they practice this, the better they get at sharpening that instinct into a habitual coping mechanism.

We can think about it this way: if the one tool I'm accustomed to using is a hammer, then every task looks like a nail to me. When I am presented with any issue, my instinct tells me to pound on it. In this way, it is not uncommon for people who've experienced traumatic events as children to engage in the same behavior they used at that time to protect themselves or to psychologically survive.

Often, as circumstances change, the conditioned behavior proves ineffective or counterproductive, but they continue to engage in it because it's a familiar way of being. This will continue until the behavior is unlearned by being replaced with positive and healthy responses. Unlearning does not come naturally; it takes work.

This is true of pets as well. We need to teach dogs to use more appropriate behaviors to satisfy the same underlying needs met by biting, such as safety, protection, resources, belonging, or leadership. This is where behavior modification with an animal behaviorist is so valuable.

> All of the significant battles are waged within the self.
> 🐾 Sheldon Kopp

I still vividly remember the first time I entered the kennel with Buji. He had made it his new home to defend and protect. I would not earn his permission to enter his space without a challenge.

I unlatched the door and slipped inside, and he bristled and growled, then charged. It took everything in me to stand my ground.

Buji hit me like a bull, almost knocking me down, but he didn't try to take hold of me with his teeth. I think somehow he remembered what I had done for him and was still grateful for being saved from death row, though that didn't mean I had the right to be in his space just yet! After he jumped on me, he ran back to a corner, his back to the wall, and growled.

My heart was racing a mile a second.

He circled, growled, and then barked. Then he jumped at me again, this time not making contact. Then he repeated the cycle. Though he bristled the entire time, he never again tried to bite or lunge at me. After about twenty minutes, I eased my way out of the kennel and walked back to my office.

For the next week, I went into his kennel like this three or four times a day. Each time I entered his kennel,

Buji demonstrated his special way of greeting me. Gradually, however, his behavior subsided.

After about ten days, I could finally sit on the concrete floor with him and let him sniff around and wander back and forth without putting up his guard. If Buji stiffened or bristled, I still didn't react. I'd trained my body not to jump when he let out a loud bark, though my insides hadn't gotten the memo.

Whenever Buji softened or lay near me, I rewarded him with praise and treats. I found Buji responded well to food. After a week and a half, he was letting me scratch him behind the ears without voicing any protests. He was finally starting to trust me.

> Quiet the chatter in your mind and attempt to simply be, not do. For being will tell you all that doing ever hoped to know.
> 🐾 Toe-Toe, the six-toed cat from Kansas

During this time in the kennel with Buji, I became confident that he had been not only abused but also beaten and provoked to take part in illegal dogfights. The scars on his face supported this theory. Someone had taught him to be this aggressive and distrusting. He'd been trained to be a fighter. He'd had some bad experiences and learned many of the wrong things about life. My instincts told me he had been tossed aside when he was deemed too old or too damaged to be a winner.

It was not a profile that inspired much hope, but each day I worked with him, hope for him still grew. I also began to notice that whatever Buji faced, whether an encounter, a desire, or a set of circumstances, he always treated it as the most important thing in the world. Though his unwanted behavior was a product of his past, his focus on the present was allowing him to change relatively quickly. As he recognized that his former patterns of behavior no longer got a reaction, he began searching for new patterns to elicit better rewards.

Nothing was going to hold Buji back from becoming what was inside of him to become. Certainly he'd needed a friend, a trainer, and a different environment, but once he had those, his focus on the moment had made room for healing to begin. There was no pretense, no façade, and his past baggage was soon just that: something in the past. He never let any of it get in the way of finding the wholeness that was really at his core, the very thing I was trying to bring out in him. It was a remarkable time of transformation.

I was observing Buji's first lesson. In these moments of sitting with him, he was teaching me to be here now.

By letting go of the past and reaching for the rewards of the present, Buji changed and grew. Oddly enough, in the patience of waiting on him and being completely focused on each moment with him, so did I. I was learning the power of presence, of being in the moment, letting the past be the past and the future have no claim on now. I was discovering how to truly be in the here and now, open to its endless potential: possibilities for learning, healing, experiencing, enjoying, and connecting.

> You must live in the present, launch yourself on every wave, find your eternity in each moment.
> 🐾 Henry David Thoreau

The magic of living in a moment is that you're fully there: mind, body, and spirit. Everything just clicks into place and is right. You know it's where you're supposed to be at that instant. Sometimes this is forced on you: for example, when circumstances are so overwhelming that the past and future fall away with the intensity of now.

However, rather than being forced into living in the moment, you can choose to plug in and stay in it. Animals do this so naturally, but for us being present takes practice. We have to get out of our own way, quiet our thinking and analyzing and judging, and open our senses to take in what's all around us.

When I entered the moments fully with Buji, it allowed him to learn and grow. The power of presence works its magic with all the animals I find in my life, two-legged and four-legged alike. It is also something I have worked into every interaction in my own life, and my relationships are all the better for it.

Living in the moment is simply paying attention with heightened awareness and not allowing every stray thought that comes in and out of our minds to take us somewhere else. We don't have to ignore them; we can acknowledge them, make an agreement to meet again later, and get back to the present. The more we practice this, the more these distractions will learn to wait until we do have time for them to exist in their own unique moments with us.

When you're in the moment, something powerful happens on a spiritual level. An energy is created between you and those you're with or the thing you're doing.

People comment about this to me all the time: "There's something about being with you. I can't really put it into words. When you're around, I just feel different in a good way."

I believe what we feel in those moments is the energy of being present in the moment.

Being here now opens doors to life's potentialities. Everything you need spiritually, such as peace, joy, comfort, love, and patience, becomes available without limit in this moment. And suddenly whatever it is that you're facing is yours to do with as you wish. It's yours to embrace or overcome, to enjoy or learn and share.

> Miracles come in moments. Be ready and willing.
> Wayne Dyer

If we will let them, if we will listen and pay attention, our pets will whisper universal truths to us by simply living their moments with us. For any animal, this moment is the moment, the only one that has ever existed. This moment is the most powerful place to be in the universe. It is complete, lacking nothing, needing no nod of approval, and ever calling for engagement.

I like to call it the principle of "Don't just do something; sit there." The challenge is simply to be with all your heart as you engage with whatever is before you.

Within each moment is contentment and fullness of joy. There is no analysis in the moment, no thinking, only perceiving. To stop and think, Am I having fun now? is to miss out on that fun. There's no pondering one's worthiness or whether you have the right to enjoy the present, no trying to make sense of it with labels or categories, nor is it overshadowed by the past moment or the one coming up.

Being weighed down with what the past has done to you or being concerned about what the future may hold is to lose connection with the here and now. These are problems animals never dream of creating for themselves. Lucky little fur balls!

> Your life won't wait for you. If not now, then when?
> 🐾Watcher, a white German shepherd in Kansas

One thing I noticed right away about Buji was that he had no fear. He wasn't frightened of being hurt, nor did he seem to have any sense of his own mortality.

Some dogs are very self-aware in every situation. They seem to be able to see two or three steps down the road and avoid any danger that might come as a result of starting down a particular pathway. Buji never looked that far ahead. He was always in the present, which seemed to allow him to trust me more quickly.

Buji never feared that I had ulterior motives beyond

any actions I took while with him. He was completely nonjudgmental and unsuspicious. I quickly came to admire Buji for this freedom from prejudice and his ability to be fully present.

You may have heard the saying, "Courage isn't the absence of fear; it's being afraid but acting anyway." Courage is a path I grew ever more familiar with, both in training Buji and in the months to come. I was respectful of Buji's ability to overpower me, but I wouldn't allow those thoughts to become roadblocks of fear on my journey with him. My efforts were eventually rewarded with Buji's trust and guidance.

> True presence or "being with" another person carries with it a silent power—to bear witness to a passage, to help carry an emotional burden, or to begin a healing process.
> Debbie Hall

Animals open the gift of the present. All they require is to experience life raw and real. They celebrate their senses instead of their sensibilities. I believe this is why animals can be 100 percent empathetic. They construct no defensive shields between themselves and us as their pet parents.

Pets are always fully present, and when we are with them they will pull us into the moment if we are open and aware. For example, have you ever been upset about something and then come home to find your dog excited to go out into the yard? Five minutes into playing catch or watching your pet race around, do you even remember what the problem was in the first place?

It's really hard to worry about something else when a dog is right there in front of you living with all his heart. It's the same with going for a ride on your horse, petting your cat, or talking to your bird. Pets pull us out of ourselves and into the moment, which is always the best place to be.

Some people call this mindfulness. Others call it enlightenment. You will see it somewhere in every religious pursuit or path to wholeness. It is the experience where everything opens to you in the moment. It's a place where you are part of it all without preconceived ideas, conditions, or expectations. A place where love happens and growth becomes our natural companion.

However, it is easy to wander through life without noticing that this awareness is available to us. Rather than living our moments to their fullest, we often allow ourselves to be pulled along by our minds.

For example, maybe many times when you have taken a shower, instead of enjoying the warm water, the soapy scent, the sound like rain, you've been thinking, *Okay, now I've got to do this; then on the way to work, I've got to make sure that is taken care of.* By the time you get in your car to go to work that day, you don't even remember how you got there. It's as if you didn't live a second of getting ready because you were never really there. Certainly your body got a shower and put on clean clothes and you will benefit from that for the rest of the day, but you were somewhere else. You entirely missed living those moments.

Each day, we trade in a little bit of life's simple pleasures for the sake of going through our to-do lists one more time. We miss the scenery on our drive to work, the photo on our desk when we begin the day, the pleasant greeting of a coworker, the taste of our lunch, and finally the comfort of the soft sheets and cushy pillow as we lie down to sleep for the night.

It's like that movie *Click* with Adam Sandler. He keeps pushing the fast-forward button to get through some tough spots only to discover he's also missed seeing his kids grow up and he's alienated those he loves most in the world. How much of our lives do we trade away trying to rush through this moment to get to the next?

BUji and Me

When I moved to Florida, I was so often referred to as the girl from Kansas that it's no surprise to most folks that I identify with Dorothy from *The Wizard of Oz*. This also happens to be one of my favorite films. No, I'm not sporting ruby slippers, but I believe each of us can identify with Dorothy's journey.

We're all summoned, sometimes even pushed, by a force that beckons us home. We all long for a place to belong, to simply be, to love and be loved and forever be free. We go on a journey to find this place but never realize it's right where we started. After all, "There's no place like home," right? What Dorothy says is true: "If I ever go looking for my heart's desire again, I won't look any further than my own backyard. Because if it isn't there, I never really lost it to begin with."

Happiness, our heart's desire, is part of who we are; it's not where we are, who we are with, or what we are doing. As Jimmy Buffett sings, it's always good to "take the weather with you." If we can stay in each moment, I predict "somewhere over the rainbow" is now.

We would all benefit from the reminder that there's no place like the place where we find ourselves right here right now. The here and now is the place we are all trying so hard to reach. When we realize the journey is the destination, we can stop traveling to faraway lands outside our own backyards. When we stop trying to get somewhere else and simply decide to be home where we are, we experience the contentment we were chasing but never realized we already had.

We can create all the flying monkeys and witches and gatekeepers we can imagine between us and where we want to be, but it won't change the fact that we already have our place in the universe connected with everyone and everything around us. We'll see it if we just open our eyes and wake up from the dream. The mere fact that we are here at all is everything that we need to belong.

Sometimes I think that throughout *The Wizard of Oz*, Toto was the only one who ever really had a clue about what was going on. He was never so distracted by expectations or desires to be someplace else that he missed what was really important: the man standing behind the curtain, the bucket of water that was their salvation, or the adventure at hand, no matter how frightening.

For Toto, every moment held a marvelous experience and truth, but all the others were too preoccupied with their own shortcomings to see any of it. The Tin Man had always had a heart, the Scarecrow already had a brain, the Lion had always held courage within, and Dorothy had already been home, the happiest place she could ever be.

I believe the characters are symbolic of the mind (Scarecrow), the body (Lion), and the spirit (Tin Man) all working together in the here and now. They exemplify the incredible power that exists within us when we allow the three to live in harmony in each and every moment.

Throughout the years, the animals I've worked with and their pet parents have been my Scarecrow, Tin Man, Lion, and Wizard to further me down my life's road. They've taught me the importance of being in the moment and living to the fullest. They've been reminders of the importance of looking in the mirror and accepting myself without judgment, living what I believe with passion and purpose.

In the days ahead, I would learn Buji's second lesson: *be true.*

Paws and Reflect

Go for a walk or sit quietly outside or near a window with your pet. Give your mind a rest and just be. Notice the colors of nature, the breeze on your skin, the feel of the sun, rain, or snow. Listen to the birds, crickets, or wind. Use all your senses and notice how peaceful you are in this moment.

3
Be True:
The Power of Congruence

Be true to yourself. There's no need to hide. When you put down your mask, you let others inside.
🐾Buji

After several weeks of working with Buji at home, he had grown comfortable with his Maltipoo pack and me. I felt we had made real progress, so I took him to a dog park to socialize.

It was a huge mistake.

Buji's progress at home with his pack didn't mean he was ready to hang out with just anyone. I was being grossly overoptimistic about his progress.

In the first few minutes off leash, Buji happily greeted the other dogs and joined them as they chased a tennis ball. After some time a sheepdog, looking more like a big mop with legs, lumbered through the front gate to join the pack. The minute Buji set eyes on him, he was off as if he had been shot out of a cannon. Before I could intervene, he grabbed the dog by the face and initially wouldn't let go. He held on until he heard the sound of my voice, then immediately released the dog and cowered as if he was waiting to be punished.

Luckily, the sheepdog was not badly injured, but it was a horrific event. To make matters worse, the sheepdog was a show dog. I paid for the cosmetic surgery to have his face repaired, and Buji and I went back to the drawing board.

I wondered once more, *What did I get myself into?* But I knew it was my fault. My overconfidence in his progress had put him in an uncomfortable situation. I would not make the same mistake again.

> Change is not a process for the impatient.
> Barbara Reinhold

It would be another six full months before I could see, behaviorally, that Buji could be fully trusted around other people and a full year before he was safe to be around other dogs. I found the key with him was going at his pace and earning, not forcing, his cooperation each step of the way. As he taught me the lessons of patience and loving perseverance, Buji taught me to be true: to look at issues honestly as they are, not as I hope they are.

Pets don't engage in magic thinking, hoping that by somehow redefining the paradigm through which they view the world they will make their issues go away. The recovery process does not come only by disengaging from one's baggage but also by embracing the healing that is naturally within us all. You can't live your truth without facing the facts of your situation that need to be overcome or addressed.

Buji's facts were that he had lived a very rough puppy-hood, most likely trained to be aggressive to win fights and rewarded for attacking anything that came near him. It had to be a solitary and joyless existence that left no room for connection with others or the acknowledgement that Buji was anything but a cog in someone else's machine, designed and cultivated to fulfill one purpose only: to hurt other creatures and win money for his handlers. As such, he had been easily tossed aside when his usefulness to them was gone.

However, while those may have been Buji's facts, they were not his truth. The truth was that Buji was a sweet, intelligent dog. He had charms that would one day win the hearts of everyone he met.

Covering them up were years of conditioning, which would take more than a few months to strip away. While his conditioning had seemed to disappear in dealing with me, it would be a little longer before he could face a world full of uncertainties and not have something trigger the old, comfortable reactions.

Wholeness doesn't come all at once, even though it's there all the time. It tends to come in spurts and stumbles, sometimes only two small steps forward for every one step back until the conditioning toward healthy behavior replaces the knee-jerk reactions of the dysfunctional ones.

> Between whom there is hearty truth, there is hearty love.
> 🐾 Henry David Thoreau

There were plenty of disappointments and times of serious self-doubt along the way with Buji during these first months. In fact, as they usually do, things sometimes got worse before they got better. With any behavior there exists a phenomenon, something I should have remembered from my college courses. It's called an extinction burst, and it happens before the behavior begins to disappear. When behaviors that were previously rewarded suddenly stop getting rewarded, they will increase in frequency and/ or intensity as the stimulus that originally reinforced the behavior is withdrawn.

Here's an example of an extinction burst in human terms. If you have ever put your money into a vending machine and pressed the button for your goodie only to discover that nothing happens, what's the first thing you do? You press it again harder, right? Then after another moment of disbelief, you press it a bunch of times in a row even harder. When that doesn't work, you might shake the machine or kick it or proclaim your dissatisfaction using a string of colorful adjectives. That's an extinction burst.

The behavior (putting your money into a machine and pressing a button to get what you want) has always been rewarded in the past, but now it gets nothing, so you repeat the first behavior more aggressively than before. Of course, if this keeps happening, eventually you will stop using that machine. In other words, the behavior will disappear altogether.

This is why you have to work through extinction bursts and not give up. Have you ever decided that you will no longer reward your dog's begging at the table with a morsel of food here and there while you eat? What does your dog do when she's no longer sharing your meal with you as usual? She may start by whining, then bark, then jump up on the table. It seems to you that the behavior is getting worse when you stop feeding your dog from the table. You're right: it is and will continue to get worse until your dog realizes her behavior, however boisterous and obnoxious it gets, won't receive the reward of food during your meal. That's an extinction burst.

Most pet parents give in during the worst of the outburst. When that happens, they've just taught their dog to beg even more exuberantly during the next mealtime. If the pet parents cave in the heat of the moment, their dog learns that begging with persistence gets rewarded.

So the rule with extinction bursts of any kind is that you have to ride them out. Don't stop when it is at its worst or you will find that you've lost more ground than when you first started. If you can hang in there, your dog will learn that begging gets no response and he will give it up altogether. Then you can reward him after your meal when he displays calm, polite, and patient behavior.

According to Thorndike's law of effect, the behaviors that get rewarded tend to increase in frequency. Make sure the behaviors you are rewarding are the ones you really want to see increase.

In your own life as well, you have to remain dedicated to change to get the outcome you would like. Any behavior you're trying to eliminate will often get worse before it gets better. You start a diet, but rather than eating less you find yourself binging on your favorite ice cream. You decide you're going to be calmer when you drive, and the next thing you know someone cuts you off and you are screaming five times louder than before (and, by the way, they still can't hear you). You decide to start exercising, but whenever you have time to go to the gym, even the littlest distraction will keep you from going.

For whatever behavior you want to change, there will be an extinction burst. Instead of expecting it and persevering through it, most people quit when they run into these initial setbacks because they think the habit is too ingrained for them to ever really change. Don't quit now! You're on your way.

> The first rule of holes: when you're in one, stop digging.
> 🐾 Molly Ivans

Too often our undisciplined habits are what formed the behavior we don't like in the first place, both our own and our pets'. I'll let you in on a little secret: the key to train-ing a pet is not as much about the animal's behavior as it is about the parent's. More often than not, something the pet parent is doing is inadvertently rewarding the wrong behavior. Usually the first thing that needs to change in creating better habits for our pets is to form better habits for ourselves. Sure enough, that also goes for interactions between parents and children, spouses, partners, friends, and coworkers.

So to change any behavior in someone's pet, I have to help the animal see that he has other options besides the behavior he has grown accustomed to using and that he can make better choices when presented with the same stimuli. I help the animal see that his previous choices will no longer receive any reward but that new, desired behaviors will.

Thus begins the dance: the animals teaching me what they're about while I teach the animals a healthy, fun way to live. Then I help the parents to become trainers as well by conditioning their behaviors to help change their animals' behaviors.

Buji and Me

The triumphs and breakthroughs with Buji came in the moments when I could see he was beginning to understand me and what I was about, not just the skill base I was trying to teach him. I could read in his eyes and his energy that he was connecting with me and catching from me a new outlook on life. I could feel the shift in his energy.

It was only then, months after I had taken him to the dog park, that I knew he would never bite another dog again. I just knew it.

At first I had been using the techniques and training I had received earlier in my work with animals and had been applying everything by the book, but I still needed to go further. After the first round of training, I had realized I needed to work on the connection with Buji. I needed to be more present and aware and dig a little deeper, beyond the pull I felt to help him change. I was anxious to see a change. So anxious, in fact, that I'd fooled myself into thinking he was ready to go out long before he really was.

So I looked honestly at his situation, putting aside my

own wants, and paid closer attention to the relationship between us. He was being true, and I had to be patient and see his truth as well. When I took him out again, it would be because he was truly ready.

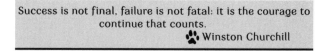

> Success is not final, failure is not fatal: it is the courage to continue that counts.
> Winston Churchill

Buji taught me to be mindful of the images and energy I let into my consciousness as we worked together. Whatever I carried in my thoughts into our training times, whether bad or good, fear or courage, disappointment or hope, I was giving it the power to become a reality.

Eventually I learned that there is more to changing a behavior than simply following a series of steps from a textbook. It is also about your attitude and the energy you impart. Positive change never came until I was truly involved and engaged in the experience with Buji as his behavior evolved.

It was when I sensed a certain significant shift in Buji's energy that I knew from that point forward he would never bite another dog again. And he never even tried. Reaching that point with Buji was one of the most challenging and rewarding breakthroughs of my journey with him.

Now it is second nature for me to believe that any animal—or person, for that matter—can change even when things look their bleakest. All of us have the capacity to relearn how to be whole.

Animals can teach us how to plug in to that potential if we are willing to be in the moment with them, living our truths versus getting bogged down in the negative facts. Being around animals and relating to them always has a healing effect on us. Even if we can't cognitively identify the reasons, we sense it on a spiritual level. When we are with our pets, we simply feel better. Wholeness is just there. We absorb their positive energy.

The healing impact of animals is all about the energy exchange. They give off good energy to those they love, and they love very easily.

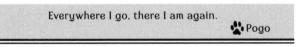

Everywhere I go, there I am again.
Pogo

It is tough to work with animals and not live truthfully. I saw that firsthand with one of my former employees. In her twenties, she had lied in an interview to get a position in an engineering firm. She'd claimed that she had a bachelor's degree in business, though all she had was a high school diploma. With her wonderful charisma and charm, she was hired into their accounting department and began a life of climbing the corporate ladder, building her career on one lie after another. She worked her way up in management to the point that she was actually advising others to earn advanced degrees if they wanted to be promoted even though they already held degrees higher than any she held herself. Over the years the incongruence of a life of constant deception became too much for her to bear.

Eventually she resigned from that company and, through one of those odd twists of destiny, came to work for me at Pet Peeves Animal Training. To process all that she had been through, she wrote a book about the experience. Here's what she said about her time at Pet Peeves:

> My current career is so perfect for me and makes me so happy that I honestly wonder how I could have missed it from the start. I train dogs. I get to work with dogs every day and change people's lives as I teach their pets to become happy, well-adjusted members of their families. I have a flexible schedule, and I work for a great

company. My boss has run the same business for years. My life is much simpler now and makes so much more sense . . .

My job is important to me. My boss, who hates to be called that, is an extremely moral person. It is one of the things I admire about her. She is the type of person who will fight the right fight no matter what it costs her. She cares about people, animals, and the environment . . . Ethics, morals, and truth drive her character. She is a good person down to her very core, and, oddly enough, she believes in me. She trusts me implicitly, and I shudder that now she will know the terrible things I did.[4]

When I asked her why she wrote the book, she said, "You know, I just couldn't keep it in any longer. I felt like I had to tell someone or maybe everyone."

She mentioned some specific things that inspired her to confess. One was a little board outside my office where we list which animals are coming and going, who is training whom, and whatever other information we need for each client. Every day I also write an inspirational saying or quote there. She said, "When I read some of those,

I thought you knew. I thought you were writing them specifically to me. They got to me. I just couldn't take it anymore." She also said, "And I saw you every day living your truth. You were so honest and transparent in everything. That got to me too."

Personally, I think what really got to her was the same thing that still gets to me: constantly being around animals. She trained dogs, and dogs don't pretend. They are real. I think as she genuinely connected with these animals, their truthfulness worked on her conscience. She saw what she had been missing in life all along and that the path to it was one of living her truth, one of leaving anything false forever in her past.

Today she runs her own nonprofit rescuing small dogs. She's always been a good egg, and she's even better now that she's hatched!

I once told her what my father used to tell me: "You know what? You can fool your mom, you can fool me, but when you look in the mirror and you can fool yourself, that's when you are in big trouble."

"I was almost to that point," she said. "But then I started this job, and I couldn't do it. I just could not live like that anymore."

I truly believe the dogs she worked with brought her

that lesson. Or you could say she drew the work with pets into her life so that she could learn this lesson from them. Regardless, in the end it was an extremely cathartic and healing experience for her to spend every workday interacting with animals.

Life is not a litter box. You should never try to cover up the messes you've made.
🐾 Ms. KittyBoo Kitty

Everyone at one point or another has been dishonest, myself included. When I was a college student working as a hall director, I was confronted with a situation where I should have been up-front immediately, but instead I tried to cover it up. I had to meet with the dean, whom I respected and admired. I was so embarrassed and humiliated that I sat shaking and choking back tears while waiting in his outer office to see him.

Dreadful anticipation hung thick in the air while I walked slowly into his office and took a seat.

The dean came around the desk and sat beside me.

With my hands trembling, I told him what I had done and how sorry I was about my poor decision.

He listened attentively, as if he hadn't already heard it all in great detail from my supervisor. Then he looked at me over lowered glasses and asked only one question, which changed my life and view about honesty and compassion from that day forward: "Wendy, will you learn more from this experience by losing your job or by keeping it?"

I paused and tried to swallow the lump in my throat. After a moment I said, "Losing it, Dean." My heart sank. I knew I had just declared my fate.

He put his hand on my shoulder and looked at me with compassionate eyes. "Well," he said, "I guess you've already learned what you really needed to from this experience then, haven't you?"

To my surprise, he let me keep my job.

Without exception, good people do stupid things, and I fall into that category as much as anyone else does. The point is to learn and grow from every experience, the good and the bad, and to choose to do something different in the future.

You don't have to pretend in front of an animal, not that you could fool them if you tried. They don't care what you look like, who you work for, how much money you make, or what your accomplishments are. They're just happy to see you no matter what. They don't care what you've done or where you've been or not been.

BUji and Me

You could have just robbed a bank and it wouldn't make any difference to them. The minute your car pulls into the driveway, they're overjoyed and at the door ready to greet you before the garage door is even all the way up. Then in the moment they see you, they instantly connect. It is as if greeting you is the most important thing they have ever done because, to them, it is. They are totally in that moment, and that moment is the only one that has ever mattered.

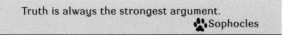

Truth is always the strongest argument.
🐾Sophocles

Even though it took about a year, Buji's transformation was still extraordinary. He went from being a condemned killer on death row to being a therapy dog who visited homes and hospitals, encouraging patients and spreading cheer. When I had hard cases with other dogs, I would let Buji train them how to behave in a community with other animals. I would put them in a training area together, and Buji would teach them what I had taught him. It was a fascinating process to watch, and as you can imagine, they enthusiastically learned everything he had to teach them.

Buji was a natural leader and now a good one. He

schooled and socialized other dogs, whereas before he would have tried to intimidate and hurt them. Not only that, but he could perform every trick you can imagine and even did some television commercials.

Buji and I had become very good for each other.

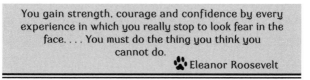

You gain strength, courage and confidence by every experience in which you really stop to look fear in the face.... You must do the thing you think you cannot do.
Eleanor Roosevelt

Right around this time, another life-altering event took place. My mother was diagnosed with breast cancer. It impacted me deeply. I went through it all with her: the chemo, the radiation, the pain and sickness, and even the disappointment when, after all that, the cancer returned stronger than before.

While it was a terrible thing to have happen, oddly enough it wasn't a completely terrible experience for my mom. She allowed the cancer to become her teacher. She gained a hopeful and courageous perspective about life that she hadn't had before. In many ways, she came to understand more about living in her final days on the earth than she ever had before.

Buji and Me

They say after you look death in the eye, you see things differently. I know this was true for my mom. She learned to savor life's present. She took the time to live her moments and not miss the wonder of even the simplest thing happening around her. She was grateful for every next breath. After she passed on, it was a trait I wanted to incorporate into each day of the rest of my life.

Of course, this was also a warning that susceptibility to cancer was in the family, so even though I was only in my thirties at the time, I began having regular mammograms and blood work done in the hope of catching early any cancer that might develop. Some doctors thought I was overcautious, to say the least, but I stuck to my convictions. I knew I needed to stay vigilant. I had learned from my mother's experience that early detection would be my best hope of beating any cancer that appeared.

Through the coming months, Buji would help me in ways I could never imagine.

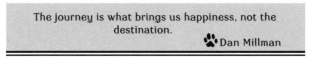

The journey is what brings us happiness, not the destination.

Dan Millman

Buji was my constant companion, and he was a mirror of the relationship I had built with him. As we teach our pets we are worthy of their trust, we begin to trust ourselves as well. It is the dynamic of facing ourselves honestly and accepting who we are that gives us a place to stand as we seek change.

This self-understanding is somehow less threatening when we see ourselves through the eyes of our pets. Because they are so accepting, we naturally become less self-conscious with a dog or cat nearby. We let down our defenses enough for the energy of their genuine acceptance to sneak through and begin to change us for the better.

When we connect with our animals, they show us ourselves in such nonthreatening ways that we're taken off guard. They cut through the pomp and show of how we want the world to see us and expose the person hiding behind the curtain, the genuinely valuable person each of us truly is.

If you think about *The Wizard of Oz*, that's what Toto did. He immediately saw through the illusion of the Wizard's fireworks and inflated self in a way no one else could. Pets will do that if we let them. They don't get caught up in the trompe l'oeil, the trick of the eye, that we use like magicians to distract others from the real us.

And often, even if we don't want to let them, our pets will sneak the truth to us. Our path through life may not be as obvious as the yellow brick road, but it reaches its goal of making us better all the same if we just allow our pets to be our guides.

After discovering that the man hiding behind the curtain was pretending all along, Dorothy said to the Wizard, "Oh, you're a very bad man!"

"Oh, no, my dear," he replied. "I'm a very good man. I'm just a very bad Wizard."

Our pets don't want us to be the Wizards in our lives, and neither should we. They know we are complete just as we are, perfectly centered in a moment on our journey's path. Of course, we all know that we are works in progress. When we can learn to accept ourselves, just as our pets accept us, then we will allow the natural healing energy of compassion for ourselves and others to flow. This is where all growth has its beginning.

I believe it's only from a place of understanding and accepting ourselves that we can be effective in understanding and accepting others. This is why I am so convinced that connecting with animals opens us to the healing we all desire. I have discovered that when people truly interact with their pets, they begin to work out the kinks in their lives and move toward greater fulfillment. Nature draws us to animals so we are able to heal and learn how to be whole again.

> In order to really enjoy a dog, one doesn't merely try to train him to be semihuman. The point of it is to open one-self to the possibility of becoming partly a dog.
> 🐾 Edward Hoagland

Something magical happens when we submerge ourselves into the experience of listening, learning to read and understand when communicating with a pet. If done correctly, there is a give and take, an ebb and flow, of teaching that goes back and forth toward greater understanding. A partnership is formed around facing life together. It changes who we are when we risk coming out from behind the safety of our own façades and simply and honestly revel in the present with our pets. This opens our perception to Buji's third lesson: *be aware*.

Paws and Reflect

Do you act in ways that contradict how you really feel? Do you put on a show for others and then hide behind the curtain like the Wizard in *The Wizard of Oz?* Do your actions match your values? Consider sharing something with a friend that you would normally keep inside. Your pet knows you better than anyone else does and unconditionally loves you, all of you, including the stuff behind the curtain. Risk sharing that inner self, and you will help others disarm and share too.

4

Be Aware:
The Power of Pure
Perception

*Go on a walk and set yourself free. When you unleash your
mind, you'll love what you see.*

🐾Buji

bout six months after my mother passed away, Buji
picked up a sudden and strange new habit. As we
would sit together watching TV, he would repeatedly push his nose against my side just under my armpit.
At first I thought he was nuzzling, but when he did it again
and again, I got a little annoyed. Deep down, however, I
had an inkling that he was trying to tell me something.

He remained persistent, but I just wasn't getting it.
As I was soon to learn, most truths cannot be seen; they
must be felt with the heart. Buji was sensing something it
would take medical science months to detect.

As I went out for work appointments, I noticed that other animals I had grown close to through training would push their noses against that same place. I would visit a cat, and he would nuzzle into that spot under my arm. I would pet a dog, and she would poke me there as well. I finally wondered if they were all trying to tell me the same thing.

I did some research and found that studies were already being done on animals' abilities to detect cancer through smell. Were all these animals pointing out a problem area for me?

I went to my doctor for a full checkup and got a clean bill of health. Buji persisted, however, so I did as well.

> Every animal knows more than you do.
> 🐾 Native American proverb

When my doctor refused to check again, I went to another and then another. All the doctors said I was cancer free, but again Buji prodded.

Months passed like this, and doctors continued to tell me I was just being paranoid because of my mother's death. They said there was no cancer anywhere in my body and I had nothing to worry about. It was good for me to be cautious, they explained, but at thirty-three I was too young to be so concerned about it just yet.

Finally, after about three months, I spoke with Dr. Gigi Lefebvre, who is my wonderful physician to this day (and I am her animal behaviorist). She was sympathetic to what I was saying and sensed, as did I, that my dog was trying to tell me something important.

I pointed out the spot that Buji and other animals had been so persistently indicating to me.

Dr. Lefebvre sent me for an ultrasound, which revealed a cancerous tumor growing in that spot, one small enough that it would have been missed had we not looked in the exact location the animals had been showing me all along.

Our pets have important, sometimes even life-saving, things to tell us if we are willing to pay attention.

A friend had a horse who had been especially gentle with her all her life, but one day she started rearing up on her, suddenly acting as if something was seriously wrong. Later that month in a routine checkup, the doctor discovered that my friend had breast cancer.

More is being discovered about our animals' ability to both detect disease and keep us healthy physically, mentally, and spiritually. It is really easy to see how the connection with our pets is part of the universe's plan for keeping us on the path of health and wholeness.

> If doctors tell you that you're in a fight you just can't win,
> then find another doctor and let the fight begin.
> 🐾Marybelle Kelly, my mom

A dog's nose always knows cancer stinks. I am grateful that Buji found my cancer, and I want to help others benefit from the same life-saving opportunity. With that in mind, I started a nonprofit called the Pawsitive Life Foundation to train rescued animals to successfully detect the presence of cancer in humans. Cancer has a distinctive scent, or biochemical marker, that is emitted when cancer is present in an individual. We train dogs to identify these chemical traces in the range of parts per trillion. This means dogs with only a few weeks of basic training have learned to accurately distinguish between the breath samples of individuals with and without cancer.

Research conducted by the Pine Street Foundation, a cancer research center in San Anselmo, California, confirms that dogs can find cancer through their olfactory senses. Researcher Dr. Michael McCulloch states, "Our study provides compelling evidence that cancer hidden beneath the skin can be detected simply by dogs examining the odors of a person's breath." Dogs have an amazing sense of smell, which is believed to be ten thousand to one hundred thousand times more sensitive than that of humans.[5]

Studies reveal that dogs can successfully find and alert for the presence of cancer at an accuracy rate of 88 percent for breast cancer and 99 percent for lung cancer. Any breed of dog can be trained to successfully sniff for cancer. A standard schnauzer named George, a standard poodle named Shing Ling, and a black Labrador retriever named Marine have all saved lives by detecting the disease in humans.

George was specifically trained to find melanoma. In one case, George provided early warning to the presence of a malignant mole that had previously been examined by three doctors, biopsied twice, and tested for cell-by-cell analysis. Stage II melanoma was found. Shing Ling was trained to detect stage I cancer and held an 87 percent accuracy rate for successful early detection. Marine the black Lab demonstrated such high proficiency at detecting cancer that she was cloned.

Early detection is one of the most important factors in surviving cancer. Cancer-scenting dogs offer us the means to provide cost-effective early detection long before the disease is apparent in a physical examination, MRI, or ultrasound.

> Man's mind, once stretched by a new idea, never regains its original dimensions.
> 🐾 Oliver Wendell Holmes

Evolution did not really favor human beings in the area of sensory perception. Human development made some trade-offs in our senses for the sake of "higher" brain functions at some point along our journey to becoming the creatures we are today. Because of this, quite often our minds work against us, trying to run every little thing through the filter of our brains before we are able to fully perceive it on a sensory level.

We don't often realize the abundance of information handled subconsciously. We might sense something intuitively, but we ignore that perception because our rational minds can't decipher it or it doesn't fit the construct of our belief system. This may explain why we miss things that are obvious to others. We have so many filters in place that much of what is going on never gets through.

Animals don't have this extra step between sensing and perceiving something. They take in more in a sniff than we take in even when we are at our most alert. Dogs and cats have approximately twenty billion scent receptors in their noses. By comparison, we have approximately two billion. This means they are able to detect exponentially more than we are by using their olfactory senses, yet at the same time it doesn't overwhelm them.

Every dog and cat has a well-developed sensory organ in the roof of the mouth. If you put your finger behind your dog or cat's front teeth, you will feel a little bump. That bump is called a vomeronasal cavity, or Jacobson's organ. It's wired into the limbic system of the brain. If you were able to examine this organ, you would find that it looks like a little brain. It's made up of hundreds of tiny folds. The way it works is that scent travels along those folds and is separated out. This allows the limbic system to interpret messages of sexuality, emotion, intention, fear, and a whole gamut of other characteristics and information that every second of every day all animals give off in scents, very few of which we humans can detect.

One of the ways dogs communicate with each other is by leaving their scent through urine marking. Dogs can determine through reading these messages left by other dogs the approximate age, sex, territory, social status, rank, emotion, receptivity to mating, and any of a handful of other little details all in an instant. It's not just a territory marker; it's more like a Facebook page or an in-box telling a dog, "You've got pee-mail!" It tells the dog everything he needs to know about whether or not he wants to meet this other dog.

> Dogs need to sniff the ground; it's how they keep abreast of current events. The ground is a giant dog newspaper, containing all kinds of late breaking dog news items, which, if they are especially urgent, are often continued in the next yard.
> 🐾 Dave Barry

When I recently visited John and Linda's house to help them with their dog Quigley, John shared a story from his childhood. His dad's poor health had forced him to retire from his job as a barber. One day, when he stopped by the shop just to shoot the breeze, one of the barbers convinced him to take home a dog. As John tells the story, he and his brothers were excited about getting a dog until they saw it.

"We waited with anticipation for our new addition," John told me. "The moment arrived and there before us was, well, it couldn't be. Had our parents gone mad? Were they trying to humiliate us? Yep, my dad had brought home a poodle. I knew then he was ill. Had medication taken its toll on him?

"I remember asking him, 'Dad, do you realize this is a poodle?'

"He tipped his head back indignantly and exhaled a plume of pipe smoke toward the ceiling. My dad was part Native American, and the chieftain had spoken. This pitiful specimen of a dog managed to slip through the tension about its breed without taking much notice of our disgust. To add insult to the injury, she came with the froufrou name Fifi.

"Fifi managed to find her niche in the family, though. She could be found at night leaping from bed to bed and hiding under the blankets with us and our flashlights and maps that marked where we had buried treasure in the woods. She seemed to understand everything we relayed to her and was up for any and all adventures. In the morning hours, Fifi could be found on Dad's lap as he read a Zane Grey western novel or watched a shoot-'em-up on the idiot box topped with rabbit ears (antennas, for you younger folks). She and my dad became inseparable.

"I think during his lifetime my dad had half the illnesses in *The New England Journal of Medicine*. Mom insisted that most of his medical issues were a result of the unsanitary environment he survived during his stint in Burma during World War II. Fifi started a strange habit of licking Dad's arms endlessly, as if she was trying to tell him something. Later he was diagnosed with colon cancer and emphysema.

"One night we were aroused by a howl that sounded like something out of a Bela Lugosi movie. To our surprise, it turned out to be Fifi. Poodles don't make sounds like that; at least she certainly never had before. Hair stood at attention on the backs of our necks, but finally the commotion calmed down and we retreated to bed.

"The next morning my dad had chest pains and had to be escorted to the hospital in an ambulance. A pattern developed of Fifi howling the night before my dad would need to be transported by ambulance the next morning. My mom was petrified at first, but then she began to see a positive side to this. She realized Fifi was just doing her part in alerting the family.

"After that, when we would be awakened by the howl, my mom would very calmly get my dad in his pajamas and slippers. She would pack his favorite western and latest *Reader's Digest* while notifying the doctor and the ambulance that their services would probably be needed the next morning. Like all the times before, she would leave with the ambulance after making sure our meals were in the fridge. She would stay with Dad until she was ready to drop.

"This continued until the day the Red Cross notified me at my Army base that Dad had gone to be with Jesus. We never would have guessed that the gift God had placed in our lives in the form of a poodle could have become such a treasured family member.

"So to Fifi, now passed, we love you. Thank you for teaching us to listen."

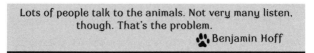

Lots of people talk to the animals. Not very many listen, though. That's the problem.
Benjamin Hoff

Too often we fall prey to overthinking things rather than trusting our intuition. We hesitate to say the right thing because we're lost in wondering whether we should or not. Our minds spin out of control with worry.

Okay, what will happen if I do that?

What happened last time I did something like that?

What if I say it and they don't take it right?

Should I really ask or just let it go?

They probably don't want to talk about it anyway.

We get in our own way and lose the opportunity to act.

Dogs and cats don't do that. They act immediately on what they sense.

Personal perception is guided by our mind's eye, and oftentimes that leaves us misinterpreting the messages or reality of the world around us. We see what we expect to see and expect to see that which we have seen through the filter of our past. Our expectations are based on experiences, associations, assumptions, and interests filtered nicely down to fit within our own comfort zone. We define our own reality by what we do and don't perceive.

But do we perceive things the way they really are? Is there a reality separate from that which is seen through the eyes of an observer? Is it possible to see reality as it truly is? Can we separate ourselves from the filters that guide our perception?

We tend to forget that through our choices we have created the details of our existence. We slip on the costumes that best suit the way we view our role in the world: the hero, the victim, the expert, the dreamer. Having successfully categorized, compared, and defined ourselves through our own little who-am-I dilemmas, we use our limited powers of perception to define the world around us. Too often those perceptions aren't accurate.

Buji and Me

Are we willing to suspend judgment and open ourselves up to see more clearly?

> As our case is new, we must think and act anew.
> 🐾 Abraham Lincoln

Being thus equipped, we face our first task. It is dusk, and
long shadows are scattered on the ground like faded puzzle
pieces. Our eyes catch a glimpse of movement in the play
of the streetlights. We squint to focus, and our minds recognize a familiar hopping motion.

"Of course," we say, "it's a rabbit. How cute!" Hoping
for a better look, we focus even more and see his long ears
and furry little tail. We can even see his tiny rabbit nose
twitching from side to side. "Oh, look! He's hopping closer
to that streetlight. Come on, Bugsy, let's really see you."

And with that, the most bizarre thing happens. With one
final hop into the full brilliance of that streetlight, the rabbit
turns into a cat. We discover that the rabbit we were so certain
we saw was actually a cat bounding after a fleeing cricket.

This is how perception works. Until we truly see,
we color our perspective with assumptions. Our beliefs
and views about the world spark our reality ablaze. Our
expectations and past experiences fill in the gaps of the

unknown. How many of our hopping rabbits are actually bounding cats?

> How many legs does a dog have if you call his tail a leg? The answer: Four, because calling a tail a leg does not make it a leg.
> 🐾 Abraham Lincoln

Few of us have the benefit of a timely streetlight to enlighten us to the fact that we don't always see what's right under our noses because of our own biases and preconceptions. We must do what our pets do and bring with us the streetlight of an open mind. In the movie *Peaceful Warrior,* Socrates says, "Sometimes you have to lose your mind before you come to your senses." To *lose our minds,* we must shut down the running commentary in our heads, which can so easily overwhelm our senses with an inaccurate interpretation of reality. That's when we can simply take in what's around us without prejudice and clearly see things as they truly are.

This is not something that comes without practice. Engaging in pure perception takes discipline, patience, and always being open to learning more. It also requires that we let go of the outcome and allow what is to simply be.

Buji and Me

In her book *Homer's Odyssey*, Gwen Cooper tells the story of a cat who at four weeks of age had to have his eyes removed because of an infection. When the author first met Homer, she was the last on a list of possible adoptive parents to consider him. Because of his obvious handicap, the rest had left Homer at the vet's, unwilling to take on the responsibility of what they thought would be a time-consuming and needy pet. Gwen came on a "let me look at him first" arrangement. She was unsure whether she wanted to venture it either, especially since she already had two cats of her own. Homer was indeed a pathetic-looking creature: his eye sockets had been stitched shut with little *X*s, he had a plastic funnel around his neck to keep him from picking at the sutures, and he was very small. However, the first time she picked him up and his purring started "like an improbably small motor," she read a face so expressive she couldn't help but say, "Oh, for God's sake . . . Wrap him up, I'm taking him home."[6]

Minuscule at birth, Homer grew to be about three pounds of sleek black, wiry cat muscle and proved to be anything but needy and helpless. From her initial encounters at the vet's, Cooper sensed an unquenchable spirit in Homer:

> I could tell already that he was a tireless explorer. The weight of the plastic cone around his neck, which went before him like the shield of a knight-errant crossing enemy terrain, made it difficult for him to hold his head fully erect. But he almost always kept his nose to the ground anyway. The exam room was minuscule, but not an inch of it went unsniffed. When he encountered a wall or table, his tiny paws would cautiously make their way up its side, an engineer testing dimensions and thickness. The only thing he attempted to climb was the chair that stood in one corner of the room, although a large potted plant that stood in the opposite corner was also fascinating.[7]

Homer was no charity case either. Cooper describes why she brought him into her life:

> I didn't adopt Homer because he was cute and little and sweet, or because he was helpless and he needed me. I adopted him because when you think you see something so fundamentally

worthwhile in someone else, you don't look for the reasons—like bad timing or a negative bank balance—that might keep it out of your life. You commit to being strong enough to build your life around it, no matter what.

In so doing, you begin to become the thing you admire . . .

Without realizing it, I established the standard by which I would judge all my relationships in the years to come.[8]

Though when she got him home Homer was confined to the inside of her apartment for obvious reasons, that space became his domain. From the beginning he was fearless, even leaping from the top of her bed, cone and all, in the first hour she had him out of his kennel. He quickly charmed Cooper's other two cats, memorizing the layout of the apartment so he could run and play with them without running into most of the furniture. The minor setback of accidental collisions never dampened his spirit, however. Eventually he could jump from a table to a couch or do other such acrobatic feats with ease and even learned to leap five feet into the air to catch flies.

One night Gwen awoke to Homer's fierce hissing, a

sound she had never heard him make before. A man had broken into her apartment and was standing at the foot of her bed. When the intruder made the mistake of saying, "Don't do that," as she picked up her phone to dial 911, Homer used the sound of his voice to zero in on his face. He launched himself, narrowly missing but startling the burglar enough to send him racing down the hall with Homer in hot pursuit. After that night, Gwen felt the way I do about Buji: that Homer had saved her life just as she had saved his.

When I was first trying to develop an openness to perception, I engaged in semimeditative practices to help turn off my thinking and simply be open to perceive whatever was around me. I would concentrate on my rate of breathing to quiet my mind and get myself into the present.

I learned a big key to listening in conversation was an obvious one: not talking so much, either to the other person or in my mind to myself as the other person was talking to me. I had to quiet my thoughts to really perceive honestly.

If you change this one piece of your participation in what is happening around you and learn to open up your focus, wonders will begin to unfold. Don't miss the journey by focusing on the destination. After all, the destination may not be what you think it is anyway.

> Whenever we wonder if we should bark or listen, we try our best to remember that we have twice as many ears as we do mouths.
> 🐾Blondie and Dagwood,
> two terriers with a lot to say

For learning to be open to the world in this way, there is truly no better guide than your animal companion. Before your pet can teach you anything, you have to learn how to listen to what she is trying to say. When I have an important decision to make, I consult only two individuals: the person I see in the mirror and the dog at my side.

"Pet listening," as I like to call it, is not hard, but it does take time and practice. My clients who are really good at it have seen it develop as they've spent time working with their pets and letting their pets work with them.

Some people have a pet but don't have a relationship. As I began training animals who were being prepared to work closely with people, such as sight assist dogs, guides for the hearing impaired, or therapy animals, I saw in them something more than just the desire to please whoever had treats in hand.

Training isn't something we do to an animal; it is something we agree to do together with an animal. These animals wanted to give to the trainer just as the trainer was giving to them. They wanted to participate in the dance of learning, the back and forth interaction, more than they wanted to master the specific skills I was trying to teach them. They wanted to see me grow and change just as they were doing. It was a communication that occurred more in the subcontext than in what was overtly passing between us as I tried to get the animal to perform the desired behavior and the pet tried to convince me to give him the treat.

Animals seem infinitely patient in trying to guide human beings down a road to better health and spiritual wholeness. It is this quality that makes them so naturally good as therapists. Their biggest challenge is getting us to pay attention long enough for them to help us.

> Our life may not be the party we thought it would be, but since we are all here, we might as well dance.
> 🐾 Toe-Toe, the six-toed cat from Kansas

Life is really not as complicated as most of us seem to make it. If we are open and aware, a natural path presents itself, showing us where to go and how to enjoy our lives. If we allow ourselves to live the journey, appreciating each step for what it is and being open to the aroma of the roses as we walk past them, we will soon realize that life is not as much about the big events as it is about the small ones.

I've come to learn that if people could just disengage their human perspective for a bit, they would see their paths reflected in their pets. Because most people aren't really paying attention in the first place, they never realize their pets' perspectives are loaded with potential.

An animal's window on the world isn't covered by the should-haves, would-haves, and ought-to-bes under which humans tend to bury life. Once we can let go of those and simply be aware, paying attention without bogging things down with analysis and speculation, we will catch from our pets more of what it means to really live. We will begin to understand the true power of plugging in to what we want out of our time here on this earth.

With this in mind, we can benefit from Buji's fourth lesson: *be focused*.

Paws and Reflect

How do you view the world around you? Your beliefs, culture, and preferences play a significant role in the reality you experience. What does it mean for you to have an open mind? What can you do to really see beyond your filters?

5
Be Focused:
The Power of Intention

Go after that bone with all your heart! Intention once
focused makes it yours from the start.

🐾 Buji

When I was nine, I went to camp. (It was my first Brownie summer camp and my last when I discovered part of the required uniform was a skirt. I mean, how practical is that really while hiking through the woods?) It seemed that everywhere I went, butterflies followed and landed all over me. I was even dubbed "the butterfly girl." I remember wanting, hoping, and wishing that they would come near me. I would picture in my mind's eye that they would indeed hear my thoughts and come to me—and they did. I never realized until now that what I was doing back then was putting forth the energy of focused thought to connect with another living being in a way that was actually tangible. In other words, I was enacting the law of intention. Thoughts are energy, and energy once focused creates that which was focused on in the first place.

As I sit quietly now watching a butterfly land on my arm and gently bat her wings, I think back to an earlier time in my life when, as a child, I would watch with fascination the life cycle of the butterfly. I spent countless summer days sitting in the butterfly garden my mom had planted in our front yard, watching these green-and-white-striped alien-looking creatures devour with assembly line precision the tender leaves of a milkweed plant until nothing but naked stems remained.

I was amazed that the leaf-munching, suction-footed caterpillars before me could be transformed into beautiful, winged creatures. *How is this possible?* I thought. *What sort of magic is happening?*

I continued to watch as they suspended their plump bodies upside down, forming their chrysalides like acrobatic seamstresses. After several days of keeping vigil at the site of what appeared to be a lifeless residence, I would witness the creatures' grand exits as they emerged elegantly winged and painted with fine, powdery colors of shimmering orange and black, the sun expanding their folded wings and encouraging them to take flight.

> We have to shed the old before we can come into the new. Metamorphosis is the magic inherent within insects. It is the magic of life that they can teach.
> 🐾 Ted Andrews

The magic of that transformation still fascinates me today. It reminds me of the importance of allowing the creative process and energy the time to develop and emerge. Sometimes it appears as though nothing is happening on the outside. However, just as we know the potential inside the motionless chrysalis, we can be certain growth is happening deep within.

The caterpillar's very cells transform, and changes take place inside even when it appears to be lifeless and dormant. The intention of growth has been set in motion, and as a result the energy necessary for the transformation has already been summoned. The caterpillar has completed all the groundwork and preparations, and now it is a time to wait, to trust, and to let go and allow the natural flow of creativity to go to work. Likewise, when we set into motion an intention for growth, it is helpful to back off and allow the process the space and time to occur.

I have found this to be true with most goals in my

journey. When we focus on what we want, we are summoning the universe itself for assistance. Sometimes the universe needs the time to work its magic. Patience is a necessary ingredient in the mixture of growth. It allows ideas, dreams, goals, and plans to emerge bigger, better, and more spectacular than we first imagined.

The belief that an idea can take flight is what truly gives it wings. I'm certain the caterpillar never thought for a second it would become anything less than a butterfly. Perhaps that's why butterflies seem to dance when they fly. If I went into a dressing room and came out looking like that, I would dance too!

With any creature, change takes time and patience. If we trust the process and lay the proper groundwork, then the universe will do the rest. It is this help that the universe promises to us all. We need only to ask. What some may call luck, I call the power of intention.

I believe the energy of the universe is reflected in quiet moments of intention. What we think, feel, want, and hope for become the energy that guides our reality and encourages our growth in our quiet places of pure potentiality. Thoughts emerge to take flight in our everyday reality.

I always knew that I could fly. In fact, that very belief gave me wings.
🐾 Ms. Fuzzy Wingsley, a former caterpillar

Buji and Me

I have always held the intention that I would be able to connect with animals and have carried the expectation that as I interacted with them they would accept me and be willing to connect with me. I have never doubted that this was a part of my life's journey. As I look back, I believe it is because of this openness and expectancy that I have had times when birds flew to me and perched on my outstretched arm or when a dog who wouldn't go to anyone else came to me.

> Alice came to a fork in the road. "Which road do I take?" she asked.
> "Where do you want to go?" responded the Cheshire cat.
> "I don't know," Alice answered.
> "Then," said the cat, "it doesn't matter."
> 🐾 Lewis Carroll

It is a well-known principle that you get more of what you focus on. What we notice most notices us right back. It is Thorndike's law of effect on a universal scale. In Thorndike's model, whatever you reward tends to increase in frequency. Giving our attention to something is a form of reward. Thus, whatever we give our attention to will naturally grow. Intention creates attention. As a result, our circumstances comply.

> Thoughts become things, so choose the good ones.
> 🐾 Mike Dooley

We tend to get more of what we focus on, of what we put intentions out into the world for, whether good or bad, happiness or sadness. It is a law of conscious existence. And because it is there, it makes a difference what we focus on versus what we complacently let our minds dwell on.

Too often we live without really paying attention to what's getting most of our attention, and that leads us to think about the negative more than overpowering it with the positive. As the saying goes, "Argue for your limitations, and sure enough, you'll win. However, it may not be a prize you want to keep."

When we remember that imagination is power, we are in a better position to choose our power wisely.

> If you can dream it, you can do it. Always remember this whole thing was started by a mouse.
> 🐾 Walt Disney

Pets seem to perfectly understand the lesson of focus. They always know exactly what they want and don't bother with anything else. They focus on their intentions. They don't get self-conscious, belittling themselves and thinking there are some things in life they just don't deserve.

Can you imagine a pet thinking like this: *Hey, will it be right for me to have that toy stuck under the couch? I mean, it's my fault it got knocked under there. It was wrong of me to do that, obviously, because now it's hard to get. Shoot! Does that mean I don't deserve it?*

No, that would never cross a pet's mind. Instead, he would think, *Hey, look! There's my toy under the couch! Man, am I glad to have found that! It's mine. I am getting it!* And then he'd spend the next half hour trying to retrieve it. When you see this, your pet's intention will even summon you to get up and fish out the toy.

Pets don't get bogged down in being self-critical about whether they're worthy to have something. They don't second-guess if they would be better off waiting for it. They just go for it.

Focused on what they want, they don't get tangled up in how they're going to get it. They just pursue it persistently and tenaciously. They instinctively know that if they zero in on the *what*, then the *how* takes care of itself.

> You are never given a dream without also being given
> the power to make it true. You may have to work for
> it, however.
> 🐾 Richard Bach

When I was still working as a counselor at Wichita State University, I came across a postcard from an island hotel near a beautiful beach with turquoise waters. I remember thinking, *I am going to work in a place like that someday.*

The thought so captivated my imagination that I posted the card on my refrigerator. I looked at it every morning when I got up and every night before I went to bed. I immersed myself in those beautiful waters and white sand beaches and even envisioned my going away party as I left the university for my job in the Caribbean. I had no more than a vague idea where the place was, only that I wanted to go there to live. It was a big dream for a girl who had lived in landlocked Kansas all her life!

Two years later, I booked a vacation to the Cayman Islands. I was so excited.

When I got to the hotel, I looked out the window of my room, and there was the same view I had back home in Kansas on my refrigerator. I snapped a picture to take home, and when I'd later compare the two, I'd find that somehow I'd booked the hotel from which the postcard picture had been taken.

After seeing that view during my vacation, I decided that some way someday I was going to work there. I began speaking with people about what it was like to live there, where the best jobs were, and how I might move there. The locals told me the best employer on the island was the Cayman Island government.

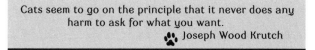

Cats seem to go on the principle that it never does any harm to ask for what you want.
Joseph Wood Krutch

When I got back to Kansas, I started to look for jobs with the Cayman Island government. Lo and behold, there was a psychotherapist position as the head of a counseling center on Grand Cayman itself. Along with four hundred other people, I applied for the position.

Wouldn't you know it? I got the job.

It may sound strange, but somehow from the moment I realized that I was standing right in the middle of the postcard, I knew that I was going to live and work there. I didn't know how it was going to happen, but I knew that it would.

It is the believing that makes things so. You don't have to figure out all the *hows* when you're certain about the *whats* in your life. If you don't believe me, try it. In fact, I thought you would be reading this book right now, and here you are!

> Go confidently in the direction of your dreams. Live the life you have imagined.
> 🐾 Henry David Thoreau

That was not the last time I discovered that the things I focus on the most become a reality in my life. Pets show us this truth time and again.

Animals always believe they can achieve their goals. I am reminded of a Labrador retriever named Trudy, who possessed the endurance to stare at the treat jar on top of the refrigerator long enough that it would summon her parent to fetch down a goodie for her.

Trudy was wider than she was tall and had intense green eyes. She had chocolaty brown fur and a tongue that seemed determined to escape the confines of her mouth. Trudy never thought her ploy of staring so intently might not work. She never complained about not being able to reach the treats or how unfairly tall the refrigerator was or how long she had to sit there gazing before she got what she wanted. She didn't mind throwing a bark in every once in a while either if her gawking needed more oomph. Time proved she was never wrong in her patience and dedication.

> Big shots are only little shots who keep shooting.
> 🐾 Christopher Morley

Then there was also a basset hound named Penelope, who was never bothered by other pet parents who said she had no business running an agility course that was normally saved for sleeker, longer-legged dogs. The shelties and Australian shepherds never breathed a word of discouragement or even howled in laughter as she stumbled on her ears, lumbering through the tunnels and dragging her tummy, barely clearing the jumps.

Penelope's pet parent was sometimes embarrassed to take her, but each time she saw the excitement in her eyes at the prospect of going, she ignored those who told her a basset hound would never be able to finish such a course.

Penelope demonstrated how the sheer enjoyment of doing something can very well make it worth the sideways glances. She wasn't the fastest on the course, but she focused on the task at hand and the rest took care of itself. Penelope's tail wagged more than the tongues of her critics.

Seeing this exuberance time after time, Penelope's parent decided she would take a chance too. She finally gave up her profitable but deathly boring job as an accountant and started a new career teaching math, something she loved and had wanted to do all her life. What mattered most to her wasn't getting to the end of the course with the most money; it was having the most fun and fulfillment as she made it to the end.

> Life does not happen to us; it happens from us.
> 🐾 Mike Wickett

In the same way, when you put your intentions out there, things will begin to fall into place so you can achieve your desires. As you persist and work and stay focused, things will happen in your favor. People will come out of nowhere to help you. You don't have to figure it all out. The universe will just naturally line up to draw your desires to you if you will stay positively engaged in pursuing them.

I have always wanted to share the lessons I have been fortunate enough to learn from the animal teachers in my life, particularly Buji. I didn't know how or when it would happen, but I believed with all my heart that it would. I trusted that intention, and then one day a client, who is now a dear friend, asked me if I was interested in writing a book about my philosophy and the lessons I've learned on my journey with animals. She just happened to work in publishing.

It was amazing, and I knew from the moment I met her and worked with her animals that she too shared the ability to hear and learn from them. The energy that was created by my focused intention and her appreciation and unique ability to understand animals are the reasons you have this book in your hands today.

> Collect your energy and focus your power on wondrous and magical acts.
> 🐾 Rob Schouten

There are no coincidences. There are only intentions that have manifested their way back to fulfill our original thoughts.

I am not saying that there won't be setbacks along the way or that this is some kind of magical formula to solve all your problems. We still have to live the adventure between where we are now and where we want to be, and there is some real work to be done between points A and B as well as points C, D, and L, M, N, O, P down the road.

I learned that with Buji. Yes, I put the intention out

there for Buji to be a healthy and social dog instead of a threat to others, but that didn't mean everything was better in just a few weeks. I jumped the gun in taking him to that dog park too soon and paid the price for it.

Few worthwhile breakthroughs happen overnight, but as we clarify our intention and then continue to pay attention, the thing we desire has a way of breaking through to reach us. It is always good to remember that the setbacks we experience often prove to be the moments that beg the opportunity to teach us if we will only let them.

A goal without a plan is merely a wish.
🐾 J. P. Kelly

We can never give up. Had I given up on Buji after he bit that dog on the muzzle, I would have been changing my intention of helping him come to a place of healing. Then Buji would not have gotten better. The change I was after never would have taken place. The incredible dog in Buji would have remained hidden. I would have gotten just what I believed in: an irredeemable Buji. Even though in reality that wasn't who he was, it would have been my truth if I'd chosen to give it the power of belief.

That belief would have cost me my life.

Buji and Me

Research has shown that what you focus on, what you think, what you visualize, can affect your health even in a very short time. When I was in college, a professor told my sociology class about an interesting experiment that demonstrates this well.

One day a man went to work, and his secretary said, "Are you okay? Are you feeling all right? You look a little peaked. Are you sure you should have come to work today?"

The man responded, "Of course! I'm fine. No problem," but a thought had been planted in his mind that things might not be okay.

Later a couple of others and a client, all part of the experiment, said similar things to him: "Did you have a rough night? Are you okay? You look a little like—wow, do you want to reschedule and meet another time when you're feeling better?" Everyone he ran into commented that he didn't look so well.

By the time the morning ended and the lunch hour rolled around, the man went home sick. He was even throwing up and had a fever!

What we think can become real more quickly than we realize. Thoughts are energy. They are things, and they have substance. We listen to what we believe, and it changes us and what is around us. Thoughts send out an almost magnetic energy that draws the objects of their focus to us. What you think is what you get.

Words increase the potency of our thoughts. If we stay positive, if we train our minds on positive things, then positive things will be attracted to us. If we dwell on the negative, they just seem to happen again and again, sending us in a downward spiral.

That is part of the reason why people who have pets live longer. It is hard to be negative with the constant unconditional love of a pet flowing to you. When we interact with animals, when we experience their ongoing positive regard and unflappable affection, we can do nothing but be more optimistic.

As I mentioned, when we interact with pets, our blood pressure drops and our serotonin and dopamine levels increase. Our happiness factors rise. As we connect with animals, we tend to let everything else go. The past and future are set on the shelf as we enter into the wholeness of the moment. Our focus on the present brings us health.

> No matter how little money and how few possessions you own, having a dog makes you rich.
>
> Louis Sabin

Animals bring change into our lives in so many important ways. Buji taught me the power of an optimistic perspective. When I was diagnosed with cancer, I had to focus on the moments I had and be courageous in the face of what I had formerly feared. That confidence was something I had seen in Buji while I had trained him, an assurance that could embrace each new moment and see its potential for wholeness.

Healing can never come from the past or be postponed into the future. It can only happen through what you do here and now. The only time you have to change is the time in your hand. If you can continually focus in each moment, then you can form new, healthier habits within a matter of weeks.

Your every tomorrow is determined by what you do right now. When you face your fears, you render them powerless. You strip away their ability to continue to terrorize you. Think positive thoughts, watch positive

TV programs, read positive books, have positive conversations, post positive quotes around your house, and positive change will come.

> Imagination is more important than knowledge. For knowledge is limited to all we now know and understand, while imagination embraces the entire world and all there ever will be to know and understand.
> 🐾 Albert Einstein

As I faced a wide array of cancer treatments, I knew from what my mother had gone through and what I'd learned while training Buji that medicine is not enough. You have to also plug the power of your soul and your mind into making the healing process complete.

With each session, I had to hook up my energy and expectations to getting better. I chose to imagine the medicine working in my body even as it made me sick to my stomach and unable to stand. I had to live in those nauseous moments, fully participate in them, and focus on what I wanted to get out of them.

As I did, I got better at being whole. Even when death threatened, life filled and overpowered each moment. During the worst suffering I experienced, I learned to appreciate every second along the way, staying in those moments and letting the healing be done.

Buji and Me

I can't tell you how much it meant to have Buji there with me as I lay on my couch or in my bed. He never left my side or complained. He never asked, "What will you do if the treatment doesn't work?"

In the same way I had sat on the floor with him in his kennel and taught him there was no need to attack everything that moved, he sat with me and reassured me that healing was taking place. And he did it with infinitely more patience than I'd had with him. He knew I needed him as much as he had needed me.

How wrong I'd been in assuming I was the one who rescued him! It was really the other way around. Together, we would beat death: once for him and three times for me as I healed, battled the disease, and then healed again. I know in my heart that my connection with him is a big part of why I am alive today.

Healing comes easier when we recognize and accept whatever

we are feeling or sensing in the moment, good or bad, and let that emotion run its course without letting it rule our lives or trying to bury it in some back closet of our souls. We can feel angry and still act lovingly. Under stress, we can choose to tap into our own inner tranquility.

Trying to escape our emotions can do more harm than the momentary relief of repressing them. We are better off facing the facts boldly and then living out the greater truths that will see us through the situation and safely to the other side.

A good example of this process is grief. Grief is very real and is an emotion that cannot be healthily buried. However, it's not something to be held hostage by either.

We need to recognize that feelings are facts and not overarching, life-directing truths. They are things of reality that must be faced but should not be the masters of our personal universes. We don't have to justify feelings. We don't have to explain them. They just are what they are.

If we feel grief, then we should let ourselves grieve but also realize it is not something we experience without reprieve. It is of the moment and in the moment. We need to face it as part of the healing process from losing someone or something dear to us. We honor the emotion and also our loved one by embracing it. It would be unusual not to feel grief when we lose someone we love, so we work through the sorrow in its moment and allow it to teach us how to hang on to love even in the midst of inner pain and turmoil. Then we also let it teach us how to move past the pain and on to happiness again.

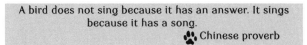

A bird does not sing because it has an answer. It sings because it has a song.
Chinese proverb

There is no better way to learn courage than to face fear. When I was going through cancer treatments, I never asked, *Why did I get cancer?* or *How am I going to survive this?* Instead I asked, *What can I do or learn or become to honor this part of my life's journey? How can I use it to enhance the journeys of those around me?*

Rather than overcoming me, cancer taught me how to be brave. It developed courage within me. It taught me how to accept the worst for what it is but at the same time still expect the best, a lesson I have treasured ever since.

In three words I can sum up everything I've learned about life. It goes on.
Robert Frost

I believe the fact that we exist entitles us to every good

thing in life. The universe has allowed us to be so that we may contribute positive energy and strength to it. By participating in life's moments, we may be happy and infect others with happiness as well. In many ways, that is the motto of our pets.

> All of the animals except for man know that the principal business of life is to enjoy it.
> 🐾 Samuel Butler

In setting our intentions out before the universe, however, we are caught in a bit of a paradox. It's easy to let the focus pull us out of the enjoyment and contentment of the present and into believing we will be happy only when we have the thing we desire. Again, our pets can give us insight into the correct course to take in handling this dilemma.

Pets, of course, aren't weighed down by this paradox. Animals remain fully involved in whatever the moment brings while still holding on to the intention for what they want but don't yet have. They express their desires, their expectations that good things will come, yet at the same time they never let those desires keep them from enjoying the moment at hand.

BUji and Me

I am sure you have heard the expression, "I'll believe it when I see it." Well, intention says, "I'll see it when I believe it." When we are content with what we already have, knowing we truly lack nothing, we can open ourselves to the endless possibilities of what could be, the true wealth of inner peace and contentment that is all around us for the taking.

If we can't find contentment in the moment, then we short-circuit the fulfillment of desires in the future as well. Intention and wanting are not the same thing. Intention is confident and expectant; wanting is dependent and insecure. Never trade your contentment in the present for anything outside of yourself or in the future. If you can't be happy now, then you are basing your happiness on something untrustworthy and insubstantial: something outside of yourself. When we can define happiness as independent of circumstances or external events, then we can embrace the value in every moment.

True happiness is something you always bring with you regardless of the weather. The storms of life will come and go, but you can learn and choose to sing and dance in the rain. Happiness is a choice, not a circumstance or a destination. Happiness happens in the here and now, so embrace it. The only moment you can ever really be sure of is now. Carpe diem, my friend.

When we focus on the positive change we want, we draw joy into our lives. That's what Buji's fifth lesson is all about: *be light*.

Paws and Reflect

Answer the miracle question: "If you went to sleep tonight and the problems you have right now were gone when you woke up in the morning, how would you know a miracle had happened? How would your life be different? What would people be saying to you? How would you look? How would you feel? What would you be doing?"

Create an Intention Poster of what you want your life to be. Put up pictures, inspirational quotes, and dreams so that you can see them every day. Check them off when they come to you.

Give thanks every day for what you have, and watch the richness of your life grow.

6
Be Light:
The Power of Acceptance and Joy

Let your mind and your paws travel light like I do. When you drop all your baggage, joy comes to find you.
🐾 Buji

As cancer returned two more times in the next few years, each time the doctors were able to catch it early enough to defeat it. However, I know I would not be alive today if it were not for Buji's persistence in warning me to check that one little spot. Buji saved my life in more ways than one.

When you have to ask yourself what you'll do now that your life might soon be over, it changes you. It changed my mother, and it had more to teach me. The lessons my mother had taught me were deepened and etched into my soul as I went through my treatments. I learned to take the time to notice what was happening around me:

the power of living and experiencing the peace and grace alive within each moment. I found myself paying attention as I never had before.

All along the way, Buji was a loving, saving soul who taught me how to travel light on my life's journey. Extra bags always cost you. Not traveling light physically, emotionally, or spiritually will leave you traveling with a heavy heart.

Do you have the ability to drop everything at an instant's notice and participate in whatever is happening around you? Animals know how to let go and squeeze the fun out of the fundamental elements of life. In other words, they know how to be light.

> My dog is usually pleased with what I do because she is not infected with the concept of what I "should" be doing.
> 🐾 Lonzo Idolswine

After treatments, I would come home to Buji and be trapped on the couch with nausea and fatigue as the medicine or radiation did its work. It was the first time in my life I hadn't been busy. I couldn't be. It didn't take me long to get bored with watching TV, and I couldn't concentrate to read. With new eyes, I lay there and watched Buji.

I noticed consistencies in Buji's behavior and demeanor

that demonstrated his love for me and the world around him. I soon learned he had more to communicate than warnings if I would pay attention. He wanted to teach me how to suck the joy out of life the same way he sucked the marrow out of a bone.

As I watched him, I became an eager pupil. Buji rose to the challenge of entertaining me every time.

> Laughter is the shortest distance between two souls.
> 🐾 Victor Borge

Buji began to teach me things only pets know. Whatever he was doing, he did it with all his heart and soul and mind all at once. He threw himself into whatever was before him.

When I fed him, he showed me how to appreciate and give thanks for every morsel of food. I have never seen anyone eat with that kind of gusto.

If I let him out into the backyard, he showed me the wonder and adventures of that small parcel I had come to take for granted, whether he was barking at birds or searching the bushes in hopes of finding something to chase or chew. He loved to put on his own version of Ben-Hur's famous chariot race, running in circles until I was sure he was dizzy. One time he found a gecko on the porch. He stalked it like a panther, perplexed at where it might be going and what it could possibly be doing on his turf. Then he expressed his loud disapproval when it scampered up a wall to avoid being further prodded by his nose.

> In the depth of winter, I finally learned that within me lay an invincible summer.
> 🐾 Albert Camus

Buji overflowed with wonder, joy, and enthusiasm. It was hard not to catch some of that lightness from him and let it work its good on my queasy insides. Buji showed me that very few things in life are more important than facing our trials and challenges with a vibrant sense of humor, never being far from the joy just below the surface of everything around us. This attitude has the ability to infect others while at the same time healing us. Buji overflowed with light in every moment we spent together.

> The great pleasure of a dog is that you may make a fool of yourself with him and not only will he not scold you, but he will make a fool of himself too.
> 🐾 Samuel Butler

Buji and Me

Throughout these moments with Buji, I could tell he wasn't thinking about his past abuse or worrying about where his next meal might come from or how foolish someone watching might think he was. He wasn't carrying any baggage. He was just fully living. As I watched him, for a brief time I forgot about feeling so ill and weak and took in the universe through his eyes.

After he'd pointed out my cancer and I'd tried to brush him off, I decided I was now going to watch more carefully for his signals. As I did, he taught me to listen and be aware of everything around me.

Through all this, Buji also taught me not to take myself so seriously. Being a little bit of an overachiever a good portion of my life, I was used to being preoccupied with what I needed to do next to keep up with my goals. At one appointment, I would already be planning the next. I was always striving for the next achievement I could check off my to-do list.

Buji sat and looked at me as I stroked his head, seeming to ask, *What do you have to worry about in this moment that means you can't just be here with me now?*

I could only answer, *Nothing. Nothing. Everything is perfect right here right now. There is no more important place to be, no more significant moment to look forward to.*

Still, as I sat at home sick, bitterness and regret were never far away. It was easy to look over my life and wonder at all I might never get to do if the treatments didn't go just right. It was tempting to be angry at my family genetics for passing along this weakness or with myself for not staying in better shape. It would've been easy to get depressed thinking over my life and wondering what I could have done better. There's a lot of baggage we can carry around when we least need to be burdened with so many regrets.

> Now is no time to think of what you do not have. Think of what you can do with what there is.
> 🐾 Ernest Hemingway

In watching Buji, though, I realized how important it was to forgive, to let go of the past, and to move on with living. By this time, there wasn't even a glimmer of the former dangerous creature Buji had been when I'd met him. Whatever any human being or other dog had done to him, he'd completely forgiven. Buji held no grudges and walked a spiritually burdenless path, which allowed him to keep a sense of humor, gratitude, and wonder.

> Only you yourself can be your liberator!
> 🐾 Wilhelm Reich

Buji and Me

Animals can teach us how to live without the baggage of grudges. In December of 1995, a female humpback whale weighing about fifty tons was caught in a tangle of crab trap lines near the Farallon Islands off the coast of San Francisco. The animal would be doomed if she was not set free.

In an effort to help, a group of divers near the Marine Mammal Center rushed to the area to see what they could do. The decision was made to try to cut the creature loose by diving in and working closely beside her, a pretty risky maneuver considering the size of the animal. One flip of the humpback's tail could easily have killed any of the divers.

A line was wrapped around the creature's tail, back, and left front flipper, and was cinched so tightly it was cutting into her skin. Four divers spent about an hour using special curved knives to cut away the rope. During the entire ordeal, the whale floated passively in the water. One diver said he could sense her giving off a strange kind of vibration and her eyes watched him as he cut the line going through her mouth. He never felt threatened.

When the animal was finally free, she did something remarkable. Rather than heading for open water as soon as she was loosed of her bonds, she swam around to each of the divers and nuzzled them.[9]

> Animals are such agreeable friends. They ask no questions;
> they pass no criticisms.
> 🐾 George Eliot

From experiencing Buji's grasp of the now and feeling the lightness with which he carried himself on every adventure, I learned the importance of facing every situation without emotional baggage from my past, bitterness about the circumstances of my life, or anxieties about what the future might or might not hold.

I learned the importance of always keeping my sense of humor, childlike innocence, and awe. Every instant, in and of itself, is light. It's absent of anxiety. It's free of pressure and all those other burdens we pile on ourselves that will never do us any good. Those things don't have any place in the present. They simply don't fit. I mean, if you can't find freedom in the now, then when exactly will you be able to find it?

If you are willing to take the time to drop the weight of the past and the future and simply pay attention to now, a powerfully wonderful world will open to you. Life is full of meaning. I believe very few things, if any, happen by accident. The trouble is that we're often too busy being people to notice the subtle messages.

There are signs everywhere trying to lead us to fulfillment and clue us in to why the universe called us to this life in the first place. If we will let them, our pets will help us open our senses to notice how incredible living really is. As one who faced death long before I'd expected, I can tell you this: it is a lesson worth learning.

> Have you found happiness in the moments of your life?
> Have you brought moments of happiness to others?
> 🐾 Buji

Is your mind always somewhere else carrying things over from work, a conversation you had earlier with a friend, or someone's slight last week? Let it go! Forgive! My youngest brother, Tim, always says, "Holding a grudge is like drinking poison in hopes that it will kill the person you're angry with. Let it go. Life is too short."

Animals teach us how to let go of life-draining burdens and be light. Pets never pass up the opportunity to go to yappy hour. They keep things simple and are always ready to change plans and respond to their environment at a moment's notice.

Pets know the things that truly matter are not things

at all. They don't worry about when the next toy will come or if it will be as good as their neighbor's. There is no keeping up with the Joneses for pets! They don't own things, and things certainly don't own them.

Animals know there is joy to be found in every activity, even the most mundane, and they will always find a way to bring it out no matter what. They never forget to incorporate a little fun into whatever they do.

Pets perfectly reflect a proper attitude toward life. They have no need to distort the facts or deceive themselves to alter the appearance of reality. Nor are they overcritical of themselves or others. They are comfortable in their own fur!

When we live with that degree of self-acceptance around us, it allows us to relax and stop pursuing the elusive sense that we've arrived where we've always wanted to be. Through the eyes of an animal, happiness is not a destination to pursue but a state to be absorbed. Joy flows out of the thrill of the chase, not the object of the chase.

You've seen this perspective in your pets. We all have.

Boomerang, one of the border collies I've worked with, demonstrated the joy of the chase. When he had the opportunity to chase anything, whether a laser pointer dot, a squirrel, or a reflection, he was off. He never really seemed concerned with catching it; his delight was forever in the chase.

Jack Jack, a Jack Russell, would take his toy and fling it straight up, then flee from it as if it were a rapidly descending bomb. Once it hit the ground without incident, he would attack it to do the same thing once more, then again and again and again. Why? Because it was fun!

When we do something we enjoy, whether a dinner with that special someone, watching a sunset, or getting lost in the flow of an idea or project, we tend to lose track of time. We get lost in the doing and the being in the moment and are just happy. My brother Tim lives by the motto that "if it's worth doing, it's worth overdoing." I can appreciate and admire his ability to squeeze every last bit of fun out of any and all situations. He truly lives every day of his life.

So should you. Enjoy! Your pet is always willing to show you how.

> There is no way to happiness. Happiness is the way.
> 🐾 Wayne Dyer

Pets don't carry the baggage of hurt or malice into any of

their actions. While it can be tempting to attribute anger or spite to the unwanted behaviors our pets display from time to time, there is always a simpler, more logical, and less spiteful explanation. Behaviors are simply behaviors, conditioned often by something we don't even realize we're doing. And they're easily changed if we take off the lenses of our human perspective long enough to look at things through the eyes of our pets.

For example, a woman from Kansas contacted me about her white German shepherd puppy named Karma. He was a bright pup and had been a quick study in almost everything she'd taught him, including potty training. However, Karma had developed the strange habit of doing his business right in front of her dresser, which was only a few feet from the door to the backyard.

As this behavior continued and she couldn't seem to change it, the woman was beside herself trying to correct it. Why had he stopped going to the door to be let out? She'd done everything right, consistently praising and rewarding him with special treats whenever he did his business outside. She hadn't scolded him when he'd had a mishap here and there. She'd learned that negative attention is still, after all, attention and can contribute to further problems. His potty training had been nearly flawless, but for some reason he was now ignoring what she'd taught him, or so she thought.

She told me over the phone, "He must be doing this to get back at me for some reason. He knows it's wrong. He puts his ears back and slinks away when I catch him doing it. He knows to go outside. He's just being defiant."

Understanding that pets aren't vengeful, I asked more about the specifics of the behavior and the environment in which it was being done. I wanted to try to get the perspective of the animal so I could decode the behavior.

Through our conversation, I discovered that she had recently decided to relocate the treat jar to the top of her dresser. This jar contained the special treats she had first used to potty train Karma.

Hmmm. "Let's look at this from Karma's perspective," I said. "He learned to do his business in close proximity to the treat jar. When the jar was located outside, he was able to keep an eye on it during his potty routine. He learned an associational cue about the special treat he got during potty training. He was positively rewarded with a special treat for pottying in the past and also learned the sequence of events that occur with each potty. Since the treats were moved from outside to inside, Karma reasoned he needed to move his potty spot inside, where he could still see the jar and would have the best chance of not missing out on the reward. He doesn't realize that where he is going is problematic or why you are scolding him for doing what he was taught."

Karma's behavior had nothing to do with revenge or defiance. Part of being light is letting go of judgments. When Karma's parent lightened her perspective by letting judgment go, she could see Karma's point of view. It made perfect sense from his perspective and from a behavioral standpoint. When she could understand the behavior from Karma's point of view, the problem was easily solved. Karma was immediately back on track. Now that's "Good Karma."

> What we believe, we create. This is the power of the self-fulfilling prophecy.
> 🐾 Diane Dreher

Pets don't filter the world through preconceptions or stereotypes. They love unconditionally. It's only when we can do this that the possibilities of being alive open up without limit.

I believe people find their paths through life when

they feel the power that comes from this kind of genuine openness to the universe. However, it can be challenging to come into each new situation without the baggage of judgment and the prejudices of past experience. Some people have so many defenses up most of the time that a lot of cutting away and cutting through must happen before things can get real.

Pets, however, are never anything less than genuine. They simply accept their world as it is and enjoy whatever adventure it brings.

This is one of the reasons looking at things behaviorally is so refreshing. Behaviorists look at conditioning without prescribing motive. I don't like hearing labels like *good dog* and *bad dog* concerning pets' overall personalities because pets aren't really good or bad, though they may do things we like or things we don't like.

Every behavior is simply a response to a certain set of conditions in the environment and is never a moral decision on the part of the pet. If we will take a step back and not judge, we can see the cause and effect of various types of behavior and respond accordingly. We can change the stimulus or else recondition (train) the animal to have a different response to the conditions that elicit the behavior.

Calling a behavior dysfunctional is also a judgment I like to avoid. Behaviors are what they are. To pets, they are simply a useful response they learned to protect themselves or get something they needed to survive.

If we can understand the reasons behind an animal's behavior, then we can resist the urge to label and judge it. We come to realize that the values of right and wrong, good and bad, have no place in the healing process. This is why I don't like to say we rehabilitate animals as much as we teach them to trust again.

We teach pets that unacceptable behaviors are not needed to cope with their world. Once they have learned that, they are naturally open to finding behaviors that will work, behaviors that are rewarded. It becomes clear to us that there was never really any malice in their actions, just conditioned behaviors created by an unfortunate set of circumstances. Change the circumstances or change the response, and you begin to see pets as they truly are: creatures seeking, just like you and me, to love and be loved.

Of course, with humans this is somewhat more complicated because we have a tendency to carry into the present hurts, patterns, and prejudices we've learned in the past. We feel an emotion, such as anger, and we react as our environment dictated we should when we were growing up.

The thing is, no two people respond exactly the same to any one emotion. One person becomes angry and starts breaking things, another buries the emotion deep inside and says nothing, another screams and yells, and yet another counts to ten and calms down.

There should be no translation required for us to interact with whomever we are near or whatever is before us. The goal of wholeness is to be able to be present with someone experiencing that emotion without the need to judge, to label, or to persuade. The goal is to let go of our desire to control and to accept the moment as complete and perfect just as it is. Then the universe will open up to us its limitless possibilities. That is true freedom.

> I love a dog. He does nothing for political reasons.
> 🐾 Will Rogers

Something magical happens when we submerge ourselves in the experience of listening and learning to understand when communicating with a pet. If done correctly, there is a give and take, an ebb and flow, toward greater understanding. We learn from their example how to embrace the lessons available in each moment.

There is nothing I can teach pets that they don't already know. Dogs already know how to sit, come, lie down, or stay. They have learned to do all that on their own. They know it instinctively. We just teach them the symbolic meaning of the behavior in a manner consistent with their actions, training them to understand human language and gestures so they can understand and respond in a manner that is reinforced or rewarded. Then we need to listen and communicate in a consistent, well-timed, and positive way to help our pets understand and respond to the messages. It's a shared language that builds a relationship as each listens to the other.

A partnership is formed when we face life together with our pets. It changes who we are when we risk letting go of our baggage to simply revel in the present with them.

In my work as an animal behaviorist, I've found that Buji's lessons are not unique to him, though there are different nuances of them in each pet-parent relationship. I've seen that pet parents who truly engage with their pets get something beyond mere companionship. If they are open, they catch characteristics and attitudes from their pets that make them more self-actualized human beings.

Buji and Me

They become kinder, gentler, and capable of pulling more of what they want out of life. In a sense, they learn lessons for living the happy, fulfilled, smell-the-roses kind of life we all long for. They learn to be light, and as you do too, you'll see that traveling light in thought, action, and deed makes the trip worth the ride.

Releasing our past baggage and expectations is the key to fulfilling our potential as individuals. When we're able to come to each situation and allow it to inform us, then the number of responses we can have to that situation is limitless. We can learn to love, show kindness, talk things through, and react to challenges in more constructive ways.

Finally, traveling light allows us the opportunity to share that lightness with others. We can always choose to skip, sing, laugh, and dance our way through life. We can decide to share more happiness rather than continued hurt and misunderstanding. Once we open up those choices, we take the limits off what we can accomplish in the world and life becomes the adventure it was always meant to be. Then we're so much better prepared to live out Buji's sixth lesson: *be kind*.

Paws and Reflect

What gives you the same thrill your dog experiences when you pick up her leash? What makes you laugh until you cry? What do you need to do to let go of past hurts that keep you from feeling joy in the present? Forgive, laugh, and enjoy your journey. Do one thing for yourself today that's just plain fun.

7
Be Kind:
The Power of Overstanding

I see you have ears. Are they attached to your heart? If
you listen with kindness, overstanding can start.
🐾 Buji

Curtis came into Rebecca's life through an e-mail message and photo from a coworker. It was love at first
sight. Curtis was spunky, lively, curious, comical,
and just downright adorable: all the things a dachshund
should be. Once Curtis moved into Rebecca's home, they
comfortably settled into a routine. She kept Curtis in his
kennel when she slept and during the day, and she took
him on a walk when she got home each night.

During the walks in the park, Curtis began to bark
at other dogs, and then he chased them whenever he got
a chance. Rebecca didn't think much of it at first and
responded by snatching him up, telling him he needed a

timeout, and carrying him back to her lawn chair, where she would set him on her lap. As she did this, she petted him and assured him that there was no need to be so aggressive.

As time went on, Rebecca allowed Curtis out of his kennel at night to sleep on her bed and even let him have a pillow if he wanted one. When she got up in the morning, she fed Curtis and then made breakfast for herself. Curtis was her baby, and she wanted to give him all that she could. However, she had no idea that her behavior toward her dog would only make matters worse.

At only nine months, Curtis got into major trouble at the dog park. He was in-house quarantined for biting a woman on the stomach as he jumped up to nip at her dog. Rebecca kept thinking he would grow out of this behavior, but instead it grew worse.

Curtis started aggressively going after anyone who came near Rebecca while they were out walking. He barked loudly and went into attack mode whenever anyone came to the door. When she opened it, he put himself between Rebecca and the visitor, keeping his eye on the person every minute. If the visitor was invited in, Curtis would snarl and show his teeth each time the guest got out of his chair. He even bit Rebecca's brother once when he stood up after sitting with them for an hour or so.

Then one day when Rebecca went out to get the mail, Curtis bit the neighbor who had entered the yard to ask a question. Curtis was getting worse, and Rebecca didn't know what to do about it. She was afraid she would have to give him up to a shelter to be put down.

Before she did that, though, Rebecca called me. I visited her home to meet Curtis and evaluate the situation. At the door, Curtis greeted me with teeth bared and hackles high. During the assessment, he charged me repeatedly, determined to make an impression—literally.

I put on my bite suit so that I could safely observe the pattern and triggers to his bites. He lunged repeatedly and sank his teeth deep into the padding of my suit. He kept a worried eye on me the entire time. His body was like a compacted spring, and even my slightest movement propelled him, teeth flashing, toward me.

Curtis displayed all the characteristics common with dominance and territorial-based aggression. Through the course of events, he had learned that aggression was an effective means to control what happened in his environment.

As far as Curtis was concerned, Rebecca didn't own the house; he did. By coming in, I was trespassing on his turf. He was the leader of the pack and was just doing what any good authoritative leader would do: keeping strangers away from those he protected. He had decided no one was allowed to enter the house, let alone even think about getting close to his pack member, Rebecca.

Even if Rebecca allowed that doorbell to trick her into letting someone in, Curtis certainly wasn't going to let the intruder move around freely once inside. His behavior had the added benefit of scoring plenty of reward from his pack in the form of attention, which he saw as an endorsement for his superior guarding ability. The more he practiced that aggressiveness, the better he got at it.

> Love of animals is a universal impulse, a common ground on which all of us may meet. By loving and understanding animals, perhaps we humans shall come to understand each other.
> 🐾 Dr. Louis J. Camuti

Though Rebecca felt she was at the end of her rope, I told her I could help. I could see how much Rebecca loved Curtis, and I knew he could learn new behaviors to replace those that were causing her so much grief. For that to happen, Rebecca needed to be the leader of the pack. She had to teach Curtis to respect her kind leadership and take his place as her supporter in a manner she approved, not the other way around.

Rebecca needed to learn to be the positive leader Curtis so desperately needed. In that process, she would learn for herself new ways of being.

When the two came to our offices, I gave them a tour. I introduced Rebecca to John, the trainer I had selected to work with Curtis. Then Rebecca left him with us for a seven-day training program. John and I would work with Curtis each day and touch base with Rebecca each night to let her know how things were going.

Curtis learned a new command each day. By the end of the seven days, he'd learned hand signals and voice commands for sit, down, wait, stay, come, heel, and leave it.[10]

Then John and I went to Rebecca's house to teach her how to reinforce the commands with Curtis and what to expect. We practiced with her until she felt comfortable and could see the new behaviors Curtis had learned.

Rebecca described the change herself: "I finally had a way to really communicate with Curtis by focusing on the behaviors I wanted him to do. He was getting attention for good behavior, and he actually seemed to enjoy it. I was so, so happy—happier than I had been in a long time. I hadn't realized what a toll this was taking on my relationships and me. I even hugged John and Wendy when they left that day with my promise to consistently work with Curtis on the commands throughout the rest of Curtis's training program.

"Curtis has passed and continues to pass several trials in his new role. He has conquered a weekend visit with my brother and sister-in-law, whom he had bitten prior to the training. I can also stop now and talk with people on walks without him even giving a growl. He even allows people to pet him, when before he would have gladly nipped their hands. He has become much better behaved at the dog park and has made some new friends. He doesn't even react to the doorbell anymore! Learning to look at things through his eyes has made all the difference in the world. I learned that Curtis and I could have fun together and be a happy family.

"I can't say enough wonderful things about the positive obedience and behavior training by Wendy and her team at Pet Peeves. I gained more than training from this experience. I gained knowledge, confidence, and skills. I gained lifelong friendships. But most of all, I gained peace and harmony for my life through the loving friendship of a well-behaved and loving companion, my dachshund,

BUji and Me

Curtis. He truly does wag my soul."

An aggressive dog can dishearten any pet parent. We worked with Rebecca and Curtis for six months, but the transformation was complete when we did. In order to redirect the dog's behavior, Rebecca needed to understand how to help Curtis get what he wanted with a more positive approach.

Learning ways to change our pets' behavior can shift our perspective about how to do a better job of getting what we really want in our lives as well. Through this process, Rebecca learned not one but three of Buji's seven lessons: be aware, be focused, and be kind.

> A dog is the only thing on earth that loves you more than he loves himself.
> 🐾 Josh Billings

In working with pet parents to correct unwanted behaviors in their pets, I have seen time and again that difficulties with animals often come from an honest lack of understanding. Frequently, pet "misbehaviors" are read by their parents as something pets did to get even with them or because they're mad at them.

I quite frequently hear things like this: "He chewed up my couch just to spite me." The truth, however, is that pets don't think the way humans do. Being always present in the moment, pets don't ever seek revenge. To truly understand the actions of any being, two-legged or four-legged, we must understand what purpose the behavior serves.

For example, dogs will chew for many reasons: to work out boredom or anxiety or to simply loosen puppy teeth. It all depends on the situation and the dog himself. From the dog's perspective, chewing is entertaining and helps him explore the world. When you realize a dog's mouth is his opposable thumb, you can begin to let go of judging the behavior and get down to the solutions. The key to understanding any behavior is to not get lured into assigning ill intent.

Determine what need your dog is trying to meet by her current behavior, and then substitute it by teaching her a more appropriate way to satisfy that need. People often take their pets' behavior personally, but what your pet does is very seldom directed at you. Instead, their behavior is something they came across in the moment, and I have seen some things that must have given pets hours of destructive pleasure! When a dog has nothing better to do, for example, a couch can be a wonderfully large chew toy. That doesn't make it right or mean we should tolerate it, but it does make it simpler to deal with. It's easier to modify a behavior when we seek to understand rather than to place blame or judgment. The same principle holds true for any mammal, humans included.

Once you're intentionally seeing things from your pet's perspective, what kind of training method should you use? The kind that's always kind.

Did you know that using a choke collar can prematurely deafen your dog? Choke collars can damage the auditory nerve that runs close to the base of each ear. Just three pounds of pressure slightly crushes that nerve each time it is exerted, and over time and constant use of the collar the nerve is damaged, interfering with the auditory input from the ear to the brain. More severe jerking on these collars can also cause misalignment of the spine. In extreme cases, the repeated tightening of a choke collar can cause eye embolisms or brain hemorrhages because it squeezes shut the carotid arteries, cutting off circulation and releasing it again at a higher pressure (similar to crimping a garden hose and then letting it go). I have seen dogs with tracheas crushed in the hands of force-based training.

But these are not the only reasons I don't like using choke collars or other kinds of punitive training. More to the point, the use of these kinds of techniques is contrary to my philosophy. I believe training should be a fun experience for the pet parent, the family, and the pet. I believe training should be enjoyed at both ends of the leash, which is the motto by which I run my business. This traditional train-by-force, dominate-to-inspire-obedience ideology is an unpleasant experience for everyone involved, especially the pet, and it is never a good choice in ethical training.

The truth is that you should never have to physically or emotionally intimidate your pets to train them. Positive reinforcement and understanding how to relate to a pet create a much longer and healthier relationship.

Pets are natural followers when you lead them somewhere worth going. You can usually convince them of that through their stomachs and taste buds! Being a leader worthy of their pack is key.

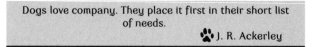

Dogs love company. They place it first in their short list of needs.
🐾 J. R. Ackerley

Pets know the power of being kind and doing what I call overstanding. This is the highest level of understanding. It goes beyond merely knowing what another feels but also involves accepting and connecting with a person from his or her unique perspective.

My mother used to say, "It's nice to be important, but it's more important to be nice." She overstood people all day at her job as a bookkeeper for a publishing company. Troubled faces steadily found their way into her office. She was not in HR and it was not part of her official job description, but she would always stop what she was doing and take the time to listen to their woes.

My mother had a way of making people feel better. Her dark Native American eyes projected a kindness and caring that went beyond any words. She just seemed to know it helped to be fully present to help others think through their troubles. They would arrive at healthier solutions on their own when given a sympathetic ear. They always left her office with heads held higher than when they had initially slouched in to see her. I guess you could say she was a natural counselor, a motivator, an inspirer of dreams, and a mender of boo-boos.

During my college years, I worked as a resident assistant and then a hall director. The university produced a monthly paper for the students, and under the pen name Dear Betty my mom was Dear Abby's equivalent on the campus scene. Responding to students who would write in with their what-should-I-dos or what-ifs, she never would tell them directly what to do but rather would help them learn their own answers, which I believe is the only path to really finding one's way. Through this, my mom helped me learn the concept of overstanding.

It is one thing to understand and plug in to the concerns of another person or a pet; it is quite another to know what to do to effectively help the individual make a change to improve the course of one's life. To understand is to empathize with another's situation and perhaps lend a sympathetic ear. To overstand is to act to do something about it; it's to roll up your sleeves, grab the person's hand, and trudge forward to face the issues together. It involves accepting the moment, circumstance, and person (or pet) while facilitating growth. It's finding the healthiest way to move forward, matching the process and the outcome in method and design, making the means as kind and just as the desired end.

Overstanding is kindness in action. It's doing what is best for another in a way that expresses the importance of the journey as much as the final destination. It is finding a place to love and be loved at the same time.

Buji and Me

One of our clients had taken some things to get rid of at the dump, and as she was unloading them, she heard a muffled mewing. Following the sound, she soon found herself digging through refuse to uncover a small injured kitten someone had, horrifically, dumped into the trash bin and had eventually ended up there.

After searching frantically to be sure none of the kitten's brothers or sisters were there as well, the woman wrapped up the bundle of fur in a blanket and rushed her to our office. Unfortunately, one of the kitten's front legs had been crushed by the weight of all the garbage and had to be amputated. She was at most two and a half weeks old.

Despite the treatment and the amputation, this kitten was not about to give up. She was a fighter and had a spirit that was palpable. She seemed to have the attitude that life had thrown the worst at her, but she'd faced it down and there was nothing she couldn't beat from here on out.

She was an inspiration to all of us at the office.

I felt a connection with this kitten much like I had

with Buji. Despite being thrown away and losing a leg in the first few weeks of life, she had a positive and upbeat attitude. She accepted the facts of her situation and rose to a greater truth, which was that she was a survivor. More than that, she would soon learn somebody out there needed her much more than she needed him.

That somebody was "Macho Man" Randy Savage. Randy and his wife, Lynn, had been looking for a kitten for a few weeks, but none of them felt right to them. Randy had just lost his father, which I am certain was like losing his right arm. It is no surprise that he was taken by this kitten who had literally lost her front leg and continued to push on. I think, on a deep level, this kitten was a reminder to Randy that he could continue to be strong and survive in the face of great tragedy, grief, and loss. There was no better teacher for him than this three-legged kitty who'd beaten all the odds.

The minute Randy and Lynn laid eyes on her, they found the animal who would help them continue on their journey. Randy scooped up the fur ball, so tiny in his well-muscled arms, and they took her home. They named her JYC, short for Junkyard Cat.

Randy told me, "This cat is tough. Nothing fazes

her. She's a survivor against all odds. We have learned so much from this kitten. She has literally saved our lives. You think we saved her life, but she really saved us."

Randy and Lynn truly overstood their new friend, and in return she overstood them right back. Helping another through overstanding ensures that you help yourself as well.

In a tough time in Randy's and Lynn's lives, when Randy had just lost his father and Lynn was going through some tough times as well, this tiny kitten had become a symbol of strength and tenacity for them. No matter what, she would not be defeated. As they opened their hearts and home to JYC, she reminded them that they could do more than just survive life's challenges; they could go on to thrive, to celebrate, to rise above and courageously tackle every moment.

> I hoped to teach what I always knew. When you overstand me, I get to help you.
>
> 🐾 JYC

Love and overstanding are, by their very nature, states of energy. They are the universal threads that connect us all in the fabric of life. They hold us together as individuals as well as letting us know we need each other. No one is unworthy, no matter what we've done or not done. There is no better place to see this reflected than in our pets.

Overstanding isn't a result of your actions; it is a result of your being. This level of kindness never judges; it accepts us as we are and encourages us to be more than we thought we could ever be.

> I know exactly what you're feeling because I am sitting quietly in the moment with you. I have no need for judgment or explanation, but please pass the catnip.
> 🐾 Toe-Toe, the six-toed cat from Kansas

When I spend my first session with an animal I'm training, my first task is to connect in such a way as to let the animal know that if he has anything to tell me, I am interested in hearing it. Or perhaps it would be better to say I open myself up to overstanding what's going on with the animal and his environment. I spend my initial time paying attention to the pet's behavior. I look at what he is and, sometimes more importantly, is not doing. I engage all my senses and try to read the animal on an energy level. I also try to perceive the dynamics and the system of relationships in the household around the pet.

In taking all this in, I assess fairly quickly what's happening at a deep level. From there, I can categorize the behavior and compare it with other case histories and what I've learned from clients over the years.

I can't start with that analysis. I have to start with what's being communicated to me on an instinctive and intuitive level. I start with what my gut is telling me. My training programs are thus always the result of a process I cocreate with the pet. All participants, whether or not they can put it into words, have input into the *how* of each step throughout the training.

I'm a participant and an observer. I first let go of the outcome and stay in the moment. I never worry about my next step. I am not trying to force anything. I am simply there saying, "We'll see what this becomes," and then letting it develop, nurturing it with gentle kindness in the desired direction but also remaining open to whatever else might develop along the way.

Like people who have endured traumatic events, animals who have been abused or neglected need me to wait, listen, and stay patient to move forward only when it's okay. After years of practice, this has become an intuitive leading. More than just a gut feeling, it is an energy reading of where everyone is in the process, a sense of whether the pet and parent are ready for the next step. If I do not perceive an unspoken cue, then I will put a little something out there and see what comes back. Then I can readjust according to how the pet reacts.

I never go in hog-wild like some super expert there to save the day. I am simply present as part of the natural process that will lead to healing, to facilitate it rather than hamper it. Therefore, I am always learning and experiencing new solutions. I am a teacher and a student in the journey. I am forever cognizant that the pet knows more than I do. This is the art of overstanding, and we can apply it in each of our relationships.

We all know deep down what we need to heal, to grow, and to move forward on our journeys to wellness. Overstanding is the key that unlocks the magic to help others and to allow ourselves to be helped in the process. Overstanding is kindness that is amplified through purposeful thought and action that serves to help others.

By their very nature, pets are experts at the art of kindness. They never judge, they forgive completely, they are always ready to help, and they love us unconditionally.

> A part of kindness consists in loving people more than they deserve.
> Joseph Joubert

BUji and Me

As a child, I witnessed the healing potential of overstanding. One day when I was playing on my front porch in Kansas, I looked up to see my friend and neighbor Annie tightly holding a soaking wet, tiny, orange-striped kitten.

Annie cried as she said, "She wandered into my yard and won't leave."

Perplexed, I couldn't comprehend why this lucky event wasn't cause for a celebration in place of her tears.

She went on to tell me between gasps and sniffles that her father, a large man who could regularly be found fixing his car, yelling about something, and drinking a strong-smelling concoction out of an old brown coffee cup, told her in no uncertain terms that she couldn't keep the kitten. "Annie, if you don't get rid of that kitten, I'll do it for you," he said. "I'll drown that damn thing."

When she told me, I stood in horror, motionless, afraid to even breathe. That explained why the kitten was so wet. I grabbed Annie's hand and instinctively raced to the cellar, the place to go when a storm of such magnitude was chasing us.

Once safely inside and after we'd both had a chance to catch our breath, Annie told me the kitten wasn't wet because her father had tried to drown it. No. She had tried to find the kitten a new home, but no matter how far away she'd taken the kitten, by sunset the little creature would always end up at her back door. In her desperation to save the kitten from the hands of her father, Annie had done the only thing she could think of: she'd gotten the garden hose and sprayed her to scare her away.

Annie told me how ashamed she felt for doing such a thing. She couldn't believe the kitten would love her despite her ill attempts to try to save her. The kitten, soaking wet, would return to her arms each time.

This kitten overstood Annie. She never judged her or left her side. As a result, she helped Annie help herself. In a moment's time, Annie learned to have compassion for herself, her situation, her family, and a tiny kitten. This kitten gave her the courage she needed to reach out for help and to also forgive herself for not knowing what to do.

Annie did keep the kitten, whom she named Grace, and her father went into treatment for his addiction and abuse. The family got the help they needed, all because a tiny kitten overstood a girl who needed her most.

It is never too late, in fiction or in life, to revise.
Nancy Thayer

Buji and Me

All my life I have been really good at helping others, though I have not been so good at asking for help. With animals, you never have to ask; they just know. Perhaps that's one of the reasons I have always been drawn to them. Animals will never let you hide from the truth or the pain or remain alone and separate from the pack. After all these years, I've learned that animals are my best teachers. From an animal's perspective, life always looks hopeful and full of promise. I believe their kindness has a way of making us feel at home wherever we are and of simply making us better beings.

A dog's tail always wags from his heart. There is never anyone more genuinely happy to see us and be with us than our pets. If we can be kind to ourselves in that way, accepting ourselves without rhyme or reason, then being kind to others is a piece of cake—with double frosting—and draws us in to Buji's seventh lesson: *be one with love.*

Paws and Reflect

Think about all the quirky ways your pet seems to over-stand you. Take a moment to appreciate your animal companion with pets, praise, and play. Then look at the world through the eyes of your pet. Do you know some-one who could use an overstanding friend right now? Reach out, listen, be fully present, and assist in a way that is meaningful from your friend's unique perspective.

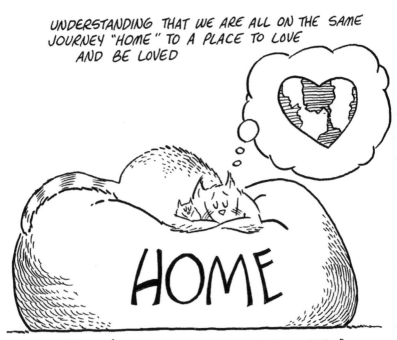

UNDERSTANDING THAT WE ARE ALL ON THE SAME
JOURNEY "HOME" TO A PLACE TO LOVE
AND BE LOVED

HOME

THERE'S NO PLACE LIKE IT!

8

Be One with Love: The Power of Connection

Life is a journey to the place where we start. If you want to go home, then just follow your heart.

🐾 Buji

The enjoyment of any journey is not merely to arrive at a destination but rather to travel well along the way. If life is a lesson, then love is the greatest teacher of all. When we allow love to guide our way, we will discover that the way will lead us back home. Our *home* is our collective belonging to the place where we share the same energy which encompasses all life. Animals understand this truth and never stray far from the place where love begins, ends, and defines their very being.

I have a client named Kem who has a puppy we are training to be a therapy dog. This puppy helped Kem at a time when she had just lost her husband, the love of her life, to a stroke. She wasn't looking to have a dog, but shortly after her husband passed away, this tiny puppy found his way into her life. Kem calls the dog by her late husband's initials, T. C.

Although we are focused on training T. C. in the moments we share, something more is happening that allows Kem to connect with others, embrace her life, and grow toward healing. As she is learning to guide T. C., he is learning to guide her to mend her life and discover wholeness once again.

T. C. and Kem work together as a team bringing hope and healing to those in need. They visit hospitals and nursing homes where the positive effects of their energy touch the people they meet.

Through the process of helping others in this spirit of compassion and love, Kem is learning to remember to be compassionate toward herself as well. T. C. is leading the way for her to connect with others at the beginning of widowhood, a time when I am certain she would have isolated herself with overwhelming grief and depression.

With T. C. by her side, she is learning once again that love never leaves us; it exists beyond this time and place. She can feel the love that remains and connects us all on this journey in life. As she holds the other end of T. C.'s leash she is reminded that the path of love will always lead her back home.

Buji and Me

Whether we are dealing with animals or people, answers always come in the connections, not the disconnections. Pets show us how love connects us and leads us home, where we're all welcome in the pack. It is only in our shared goals and understanding that things get better.

> Until one has loved an animal, a part of one's soul remains unawakened.
> 🐾 Anatole France

Loving acts are more than ripples on the water. They represent the great wave underneath the surface that moves beings. It is unconditional love, the kind of love that does not seek recognition or reward, that makes the biggest difference of all. True love accepts and gives regardless of what kind of feedback it receives. That's what makes it unconditional.

After all, trust, love, self-worth, belonging, and the like can never be earned. They are states of being that we can either embrace and celebrate or spend countless years and hours chasing but never reaching because we're convinced we're never quite good enough to deserve them.

The truth is that we do deserve love because we are love: every one of us. It is the stuff that connects us, inspires us, and brings us to the place of true belonging.

It is love that opens the realization that we are one with it all, that we always have been and forever will be. In the eyes of our pets, whether they purr, bark, squawk, or whinny, we are perfect simply because of our being. Pets exude love because it is their nature. If we fail to exude love to others, it is because we have forgotten our true nature.

Love leads the way when we focus on truly connecting with another. It guides not only where we are going but how we get there. I believe that how you do something is just as important as what you're trying to do. After all, the destination is the journey. Both what we do and how we do it are important aspects of determining our happiness along the way.

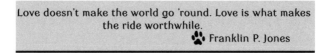

Love doesn't make the world go 'round. Love is what makes the ride worthwhile.
Franklin P. Jones

Love blooms from a foundation of trust. Trust never comes without connection and valuing the other's interests as much as you value your own. "Love your neighbor as yourself" means loving others no more and no less than you love yourself.

In building trust with our pets, it is helpful to focus on the relationship as the foundation for any other behaviors we may want to see occur. Personal agendas have a way of hindering pure, genuine connection. When we let go of defining the relationship in terms of winning or losing, good or bad, or fixing what we think might be broken, then we are in a position to establish trust. When we accept others as we would like to be accepted, then we can begin to love without conditions.

When we realize we are identical to the fundamental energy of the universe, we can let go of thinking in terms of labels and categories. We can learn what our pets have known all along: that without exception we all belong. Ram Dass describes this connection in the principle of Namaste:

> I honor the place in you
> in which the entire universe dwells.
> I honor the place in you
> which is of love, of truth, of light, and of peace.
> I honor the place in you where,
> if you are in that place in you,
> and I am in that place in me,
> there is only one of us.

It is only when we can make this kind of a connection that we will gain an animal's trust enough to partner with her in overcoming challenges. When we connect, we are actively involved in a process of playing and learning together. Certainly we can teach animals to learn new behaviors, as many trainers do, but that is not connecting. Learning should not be a one-way street but a collaborative endeavor. It comes with this kind of connection.

I have experienced this so much in working with different pets and people that I can feel it the moment it happens. In that instant together with another, I get caught up in the process of the process. When we are open and aware, this universal connection happens effortlessly and unlocks the power of all possibilities. It may sound bizarre and maybe even a little mystical, but I know and can feel this process at work in my interactions with others.

> Be patient toward all that is unsolved in your heart and try to love the questions themselves. . . . Live the questions now. Perhaps you will then gradually, without noticing it, live along some distant day into the answers.
> 🐾 R. M. Rilke

When I talk to my team at Pet Peeves, I ask them, "What is our mission? Are we simply training animals and teaching certain skills? Yes, to a certain extent, but that is only a part of what we do. The truth is that we are teaching something deeper. We are teaching the pet parents as well as the pets. We are teaching them how to truly connect, how to love unconditionally, how to listen and understand, how to be present, how to be kind, and how to just be. We do this through the process of pet training, but we are really on a bigger mission: we are teaching people things they can't learn any other way. We are helping pets help their people while helping people help their pets. Our true goal is to help make the world a better place one pet and one relationship at a time."

When we are one with love, we are home. Home is a place of mutual trust and belonging. It is where the entire universe touches every other part and comes into harmony and peace. It is where we can truly give of ourselves unselfishly. It is this place that allows us to connect to every living organism in a moment's time with all the beings on our planet. Love is the energy that holds us together, draws us close, and is a constant commonality of our being. It is this stuff that beckons us all home.

Wild Geese

You do not have to be good.
You do not have to walk on your knees
for a hundred miles through the desert, repenting.
You only have to let the soft animal of your body
       love what it loves.
Tell me about despair, yours, and I will tell you mine.
Meanwhile the world goes on.
Meanwhile the sun and the clear pebbles of the rain
are moving across the landscapes,
over the prairies and the deep trees,
the mountains and the rivers.
Meanwhile the wild geese, high in the clean blue air,
are heading home again.
Whoever you are, no matter how lonely,
the world offers itself to your imagination,
calls to you like the wild geese, harsh and exciting—
over and over announcing your place
in the family of things.

🐾 Mary Oliver[11]

If we want to occupy the space that is love and become love, then we need to jump in and not let the what-if monster fuel our fears and keep us separate from our collective belonging, our rightful place in the universe. It can't be bought or bartered for but only gained through surrendering to the moment with all our senses.

True love and fear can't occupy the same space because perfect love casts out all fear. Neither will love be fenced in by the rules and requirements that we often im-

will never ask you to be more than you are right here right now. When we learn that kind of acceptance of self and others, it offers us a healthy place to grow and belong on our journey.

When I think about love, I think about connection: the sharing, the ebb and flow of energy among all beings. It is not the type of romantic, feeling-based sensation that most people associate with the topic of love. It is about being part of a larger system that is life itself. I see this connection occur effortlessly with animals. They share an understanding, an awareness that we are all made up of the same energy. They don't try to define, negotiate, own, or leverage their connections with those around them. They connect effortlessly.

If we learn to listen closely, the questions will answer themselves. Be still in the presence of your animal companion, and learn what he knows. Your furry friend has something to teach you if you are willing to really listen. You will not find a more perfect mirror in which to truly see who you are than the eyes of your pet. Here there is no need for criticism or judgment, just acceptance and the promise of growth through awareness.

This kind of connection was to be Buji's greatest lesson for me as well as the hardest to bear.

> I've found it's neither the roads before you nor the roads you've already traveled that are important, but it's how you enjoy the ride along the way. So roll down the window and let your tongue hang out!
>
> 🐾 Buji

It wasn't long after I had beaten cancer for the third time that I began to feel a subtle shift in Buji's energy. There was a change in the connection I had felt with him since the day he'd turned the last corner in his training. It was as though he wasn't as present as he used to be. It was similar to the feeling you get from an old friend who is preparing to leave on a journey and you know won't return for quite some time or maybe never again.

This feeling grew for a few weeks and bothered me so much that I decided to take Buji to the vet. The vet understood Buji might not be feeling well but couldn't determine why there had been a change in his energy.

When we got home, Buji would just lie around and stare at me, showing none of his usual exuberance. I knew he was struggling with something. The next day, I scheduled an appointment with a specialist.

When we showed up in the waiting room for the appointment, Buji collapsed on the floor and I had to carry him into the exam room. After doing a number of scans and tests, the specialist told me Buji was in the late stages of cancer. It had consumed most of his body.

Even as I heard the words, I could sense the light fading from Buji's eyes. He was not going to beat cancer as he had helped me to. There was nothing I could do to save him.

I felt completely powerless.

Dogs are not our whole life, but they make our lives whole.
🐾 Roger Caras

Though Buji held on a little while longer, I could tell his life was coming to an end. On Valentine's Day of 2008, I held him as he took his final breath. I watched the light in his eyes fade, and I felt my heart break.

I cried and cried. I turned night into day and day into night until I cried myself to sleep.

As anyone who has loved and lost an animal knows, they take a piece of your heart with them when they go. My heart was certainly broken, but I discovered when I put the pieces back together that nothing was lost, that love never left, and that love would remain my constant companion. As I struggled to understand how Buji could be taken by the very disease that he had helped me to first find and then defeat three times, I allowed myself to accept the journey.

I had thought until I just couldn't think anymore, and then I realized what I had known all along but had forgotten somewhere along the way. Life happens in the moments when we remember that love is the state of our true being. As I played the pictures back in my mind of Buji living the moments of his life without fear of the past or concerns for the future, I finally understood the power of loving all of life's moments. I learned that love is not something to be gained or lost. It is something we are.

Every single one of us is part of one love. When we realize this, it is possible for us, once again, to become aware of this connection so we can exist in a state of harmony and joy with all beings. When we choose to celebrate each moment with gratitude for living, we allow the one love to become our teacher.

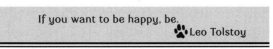

> If you want to be happy, be.
> 🐾 Leo Tolstoy

When we start to view love as something we are, as something we belong to in our being, there is nothing to hold on to or risk losing, because we are part of it all. One love, one system, one being, and ultimately one home. I knew Buji would always be with me as a guide, a teacher, a reminder to live, really live, each and every moment of my life.

> You don't want me to leave, but it's time that I go. What I came here to teach, you already know.
> 🐾 Buji

My first appointment the following day was with a family from India who had a little Yorkie named Cheeku, which in Hindi means sweet plum. Cheeku was a spirited little ball of fluff, a blaze running back and forth dragging a toy duck that was far bigger than he was tall.

I couldn't help but smile when I saw Cheeku, yet underneath it all, I could feel the ache in my heart for Buji.

The family could sense something was bothering me, so they asked me how I was feeling. When I told them about Buji, they listened empathetically. Then the man, a physician with kind eyes, looked intently at me and said, "In our culture, it is believed that an animal will take on the ailment of the person he loves the most. Buji took on your cancer so that you no longer had to bear it."

It was the first time I ever cried during an appointment. I knew he was right. Buji had not only pointed out my cancer for the doctors to treat, but when it had returned again and again, he had taken it into himself and beaten it one more time for me. Wiping tears from my eyes, I said a silent thank-you to my lost friend.

As I worked with Cheeku, I was pulled back to the magic of being in the moment with this little creature and his family, who loved him so. As I engaged in training Cheeku, I could once again feel a connection with Buji through the light of the little puppy's eyes. A wave of comfort came over me as I remembered what Buji had taught me: that all life is energy and energy never dies; it just changes form.

I knew from that moment on what I believe to be the truth about love: it is never lost, and it never dies. I knew in my continued work with animals, Buji would never be far away.

> Wheresoever you go, go with all your heart.
> 🐾 Confucius

In Buji's memory, I decided to put into practice what he and other animals have taught me over the years. I thought more and more about the life-giving characteristics Buji had shared with me. It was these qualities that ultimately became Buji's seven lessons: be here now, be true, be aware, be focused, be light, be kind, and be one with love.

In my journey, I have learned that most of life's important lessons involve remembering what our souls have forgotten along the way. When I watched Buji's life slip past this physical plane, I was reminded that death and letting go are one and the same and that the energy of life carries on until we all meet in the place we will ultimately call home.

I am a better behaviorist, friend, and human being for choosing to embrace all the moments of my life: the ones that break my heart as well as the ones that give my joy wings. Life, all of life, is worth showing up for: being fully present in the moments that shape our souls and light our lives. When I let go of my attachment to the outcome of situations, life reveals incredible lessons if I will only let them flow to me: lessons about connecting with others and finding a place to call home with friends and family.

> Living with animals can be a wonderful experience, especially if we choose to learn the valuable lessons animals teach through their natural enthusiasm, grace, resourcefulness, affection, and forgiveness.
> 🐾 Richard H. Pitcairn

When we discover and travel on our own paths, then the

paths will widen for us to discover new and different lands that will lead us home. If we are open and aware, our animals will help us remember that which we may have forgotten along the way: that we are part of it all, that we deserve every good thing, that we belong by the very nature that allows us to be, that we are love, and that love is the place where, in the beginning and in the end, we all belong.

If we listen carefully, our pets will whisper the way to guide us on our journey back home: a journey to a place where love embraces every single moment of our amazing lives. Discovering Buji's seven lessons has certainly been a homecoming for me, and I hope for you as well. Too easily we forget that there are things more important on this journey than the madness that tries to pull us away from our rightful place of belonging: our home.

Dorothy Gale, my kindred spirit from Kansas, had it right all along: "There's no place like home."

Welcome home, my friend.

Welcome home.

Paws and Reflect

Buji's seven lessons have offered me a reliable compass on this journey. Feel free to adopt any or all the principles that feel right to you for your own life. Also feel free to reject any and all that don't fit, and make up your own. Let your pet help you listen and learn what they might be. Ask the question, "How do I decide?" The mere act of asking summons the answer to you. You may be surprised at the manner in which it is delivered. Then again, that's the thrill and mystery of the beautiful gift of life.

Notes

1. Jeanie Lerche Davis, "5 Ways Pets Can Improve Your Health," *Web MD,* September 27, 2009, http://www.webmd.com/hypertension-high-blood-pressure/guide/5-ways-pets-improve-your-health.

2. Beau Hodai, "Study: Dogs improve health of their human companions," *Natural News,* January 23, 2007, http://www.naturalnews.com/021483.html.

3. E. J. Mundell, "Cats Help Shield Owners from Heart Attack," *U.S. News and World Report,* February 21, 2008, http://health.usnews.com/usnews/health/healthday/080221/cats-help-shield-owners-from-heart-attack.htm.

4. Andrea Stanfield, *Phony: How I Faked My Way Through Life* (New York: Prometheus Books, 2008), 203-204.

5. "Dogs can smell out cancer by sniffing breath samples: study," *Earth Times,* January 13, 2006, http://www.earth-times.org/articles/news/5002.html.

6. Gwen Cooper, *Homer's Odyssey: A Fearless Feline Tale, or How I learned About Love and Life with a Blind Wonder Cat* (New York: Delacourte Press, 2009), 20.

7. Cooper, 22.

8. Cooper, 30.

9. Peter Fimrite, "Daring rescue of whale off Farallones," *Terra Nature,* December 14, 1995, http://www.terranature.org/whaleSanFranciscoRescue.htm.

10. To learn more about this program, visit www.pet-peeves.info.

11. Mary Oliver, "Wild Geese," *Dream Work* (New York: Atlantic Monthly Press, 1986), 14.

Pawsitive Life Foundation

"Saving lives at both ends of the leash"

At the Pawsitive Life Foundation, we rescue dogs and train them to provide early cancer detection in humans.

Research demonstrates that any breed of dog can be trained to sniff for the presence of cancer in humans. We teach this highly effective skill by training dogs to identify a very distinctive scent, or biochemical marker, that is emitted by the human body and found in the breath when cancer is present.

A dog's sense of smell is so keen and accurate that he can identify the chemical traces of cancer in the range of parts per trillion (equivalent to being able to detect a drop of blood in an Olympic-sized swimming pool).

Imagine going to your doctor for your yearly checkup and simply breathing into a special tube to be later screened by a trained cancer detection dog. This test provides an accurate and cost-effective way to alert you of the possible presence of cancer early enough to help you and your doctor save your life.

Help us make cancer detection tests available in your area by donating online at www.cancerstinks.com. Your donation helps us save a dog and train him or her to help save a human life.

For more information, donations, or to volunteer, please contact us at:

www.pawsitivelife.org
The Pawsitive Life Foundation
7791 52nd Street North
Pinellas Park, FL 33781
727-953-7752

MEDALLION
P R E S S

Want to know what's going on with
your favorite author or what new releases
are coming from Medallion Press?

Now you can receive breaking news,
updates, and more from Medallion Press
straight to your cell phone, e-mail, instant messenger, or Facebook!

Sign up now at www.twitter.com/MedallionPress to stay on top of all
the happenings in and
around Medallion Press.

For more information
about other great titles from
Medallion Press, visit

medallionpress.com